Faith
Connections
Leader's Guide

Fall

24

Challenges for Faithful Followers

God in the Shadows

Leader's Guide

Contents
Fall 2024
VOLUME 48, NUMBER 1

FoundryLeader.com

To enhance your session preparation, check out the following resources available online.

Leader's Guide

•**Unit Videos:** You, and/or your group, will gain insight and support from the expertise of leading Wesleyan scholars. This quarter Dr. Jim Edlin introduces **Unit 1, Unit 2,** and **Session 6**.

•Customizable versions of the session so you can customize to fit your unique group situation.

•Session notes that enable the group to follow the discussion questions.

•PowerPoints for each session.

Illustrated Bible Life

•**Articles Out Loud:** Don't have time to read the *Illustrated Bible Life* article for the week? You can now listen to the article on the go with the new, weekly IBL "Articles Out Loud."

•Articles and verse-by-verse commentary for each session.

Access the materials on FoundryLeader.com using a password obtained by the purchase of the *Leader's Guide* and/or *Illustrated Bible Life.* There is a separate password for each listed in your material.

We believe in the full inspiration of the Scripture and encourage the comparison and use of several translations as part of the discipline of Bible study.

All Scripture quotations marked † are the author's own translations from the original languages.

Leader's Guide is published quarterly by The Foundry Publishing®, P.O. Box 419527, Kansas City, MO 64141. Copyright © 2024 by The Foundry Publishing®. Canadian GST No. R129017471.

See page 86 for additional copyright information.

Perspectives

Take Heart! God Is at Work

Here is a riddle: *When you fall down, it's because of me. I hold you down, but for your own good. What am I?* Answer: Gravity. Gravity is "the force by which a planet or other body draws objects toward its center. The force of gravity keeps all of the planets in orbit around the sun."* Gravity is the reason why, when you jump up in the air, you come down rather than floating off into the atmosphere. It is the reason why, when things are dropped from a tall building, they plummet to the ground. We can't see gravity, but we know it's there and always at work.

A year ago, my wife and I took a weekend trip. While on our brief getaway, we went to a musical drama based on the story of Queen Esther. The presentation included live animals, elaborate staging, colorful costumes, and talented vocal performances. As amazing as all that was, the story is even more amazing. All through the production, I couldn't help but think how God was at work throughout the story, even when the central characters like Esther and Mordechai couldn't plainly see all the ways in which God was moving.

Throughout the Bible, we encounter stories of God working behind the scenes (e.g., Joseph; Jonah). In the story of Esther, it is not hard to see God's hand moving on behalf of His people. Despite how things looked outwardly, God was at work. Even the fact that we see God moving, yet is not specifically mentioned in the story of Esther, testifies to God's sovereignty and providence. At one point in the story, Esther's cousin Mordecai tells her, "If you remain silent at this time, relief and deliverance for the Jews will arise from another place, but you and your father's family will perish. And who knows but that you have come to your royal position for such a time as this?" (Esther 4:14). Mordecai's statement points to the fact that God is always working in and through people and situations to accomplish His will.

Take heart! Even when we can't see it, or even feel it, God is moving. Today, may we be reminded that we must "live by faith, not by sight" (2 Corinthians 5:7), resting in the truth that God is at work.

May God bless you as you study His Word this quarter!

MIKE WONCH
Editor

*<https://spaceplace.nasa.gov/what-is-gravity/en/> Accessed January 18, 2024.

Questions?

- Call our toll-free number, 1-800-877-0700, Monday—Friday, 8:00 am—4:30 pm.

- Email us through "Ask the Editor" on our website FoundryLeader.com.

- Write us at P.O. Box 419527, Kansas City, MO 64141.

Prepare to Lead

What You Will Find in a Typical Session

Session Outcome: The session objective for that particular session.

The Word (Scripture focus): The Bible study for each week is based on Bible verses (NIV translation) printed in the session.

Key Verse: Each week a key verse of Scripture is highlighted. This verse (or verses) points to the theme of that week's session.

Session Theme: The underlying theme of each session is captured in a single sentence and presented as the session truth.

Engage the Word: The Scripture exposition represents an in-depth, practical examination and explanation of the Scripture passage.

Discussion Guide in Four Steps

Connect to My Experience (Opening activity to introduce the session.) This opening is designed to capture their attention and interest, and begin to move their thoughts to the Bible study topic.

Connect to the Word (Reading and unpacking of the Scripture passage.) This is the time when you "unpack" the session passage and understand what the message of the verses has to say to us today.

Connect to My Life and the World (Heart and life connections to the biblical passage and steps to apply the Word in daily life.) Discussion on how today's session relates to life and ways to involve the adults in making personal decisions and commitments to enact God's Word in their lives.

Insight This is information that will help you as the facilitator understand the session passage in a deeper and more comprehensive way.

The Book of Daniel

When I survey the children's Bibles read by my son and daughter, only two writing prophets typically receive much attention: Jonah and Daniel. Although prophetic writing constitutes a large chunk of the Old Testament, it can be very difficult to understand. Even so, there is something special about Daniel that makes the book accessible to the Bible's youngest readers, even as it baffles the most learned scholars. Considering that most of us fall somewhere between those two groups: What is it that Daniel might teach the church today? How might we understand its historical background and what makes it so special?

A Different Kind of Prophet

Daniel, both the man and the book, stand apart from other prophets in the Old Testament. Daniel was one of two known biblical prophets who wrote in exile, but also had experienced life in Judah before it fell to Babylon (the other prophet was Ezekiel). Daniel would have been a younger contemporary to Jeremiah and Habak-kuk. When he was still young, the Babylonian King Nebuchadnezzar forcibly moved Daniel and many of his peers to Babylon in 597 BC (see 2 Kings 24:14). It was after this that Daniel and his three friends received training for service in the Babylonian royal court.

The book of Daniel narrates the life of the man after his deportation to Babylonia. In Babylon, Daniel became one of the wise men and exhibited the ability to interpret dreams. In addition to dream interpretation, Daniel had dreams and visions of his own, which we find in Daniel 6–-12. The earlier chapters of Daniel report his trials and faithfulness to God as a Judean exile who served several different kings in two empires (the Babylonian empire fell to Persia in 539 BC).

As a book, Daniel has several special features. First, it is one of two books in the Old Testament that contains substantial portions originally written in Aramaic rather than Hebrew. This change reflects the universal language (Aramaic) at the time Daniel was written. Secondly, Daniel also includes several Greek and Persian loanwords (Greek and Persian words written in Hebrew-Aramaic letters), which fits with a book written during the Persian period. Lastly, the book of Daniel is a mixture of different types of literature. Its early chapters are primarily stories about the experiences of Judean exiles in Babylon (whether Daniel, or his compatriots—Shadrach, Meshach, and Abednego). The latter half of Daniel reports prophetic and apocalyptic visions that Daniel received. These visions reveal a heavenly perspective on the events of Daniel's lifetime and the centuries that would follow.

Eschatology and Apocalypse

Two important terms for understanding the prophets, and Daniel in particular, are "eschatology" and "apocalypse." Eschatology refers to a doctrine of the end times. In biblical theology, this involves the arrival of God's kingdom and the return of Jesus. Daniel 7 speaks about four kingdoms, the last of which apparently arises at the end of time. Jim Edlin explained the vision well when he concluded that this chapter narrates human history from Babylon to the end of time with the first kingdom representing Babylon and the fourth kingdom the final kingdom of human history. Meanwhile, the middle two kingdoms "do not necessarily intend to reference particular historical entities but rather stand as representatives of the kinds of kingdoms the world will experience."[1]

Other parts of Daniel seem to speak directly to the second century before Christ. Jewish people reading Daniel 11 in that time would have found parallels to events surrounding the reign of Antiochus IV Epiphanes (175–163 BC) and his persecution of God's people. Such readers would also recognize Daniel's description of the wars between rival Greek kingdoms in their time. But even as Daniel spoke to people in the second century, the book addresses God's people throughout history. Therefore, Christians are also correct to see instantiations of the beasts of Daniel 7–-8 in their own time because—as noted above—the beasts have a broader reference point than any one kingdom. Rather, in Daniel, the kings of Persia and Greece sit for a portrait of the spiritual reality that lies behind earthly kingdoms throughout history.

It is here that Daniel begins to resemble the type of writing called, "apocalypse." Designating Daniel as apocalyptic fires the imagination for modern readers. When we hear the word "apocalypse," we imagine cataclysmic events that create a horrific dystopia while history as we know it careens out of control. Although that may be one meaning of the word "apocalypse" in our modern vernacular, when biblical scholars use the term they are referring to a specific type of writing. Just as a piece of modern literature might be a newspaper, novel, or a Sunday School curriculum introductory article, one type of writing in the ancient world was called "apocalypse."

Defining any genre of literature proves difficult, but apocalypses have a number of common characteristics. They typically include a story about an individual who sees a vision, which is in turn interpreted, often by some sort of angelic visitor or vision-guide. The second half of Daniel contains each of these characteristics. Another feature of apocalypses is that they typically pertain to the writer's present, or to the not too distant future. This is where Daniel can become a little tricky. For example, the events symbolized in Daniel 11:5–45 narrate—with precision at several points-—the history of the Greek kingdoms that arose following Alexander the Great's death. This would be long after Daniel-the-man had died and would make Daniel-the-book a special example of apocalyptic writing that is predictive of events centuries down the road if one concludes Daniel-the-man wrote the book.

That point aside, for Jewish people reading Daniel in the second century before Christ, Daniel was no newspaper from the future that reported events millennia beforehand. Rather, they recognized an important feature of biblical apocalypses: apocalyptic literature speaks to God's people now, whenever "now" might be. While apocalypses, by their nature, address the future, their primary reason for doing so is to encourage faithfulness amongst God's people in the present. Thus, it is important for us now to consider the message and theology of Daniel.

The Message and Theology of Daniel[2]

God is Sovereign

Theologically, Wesleyan-Arminian readers can become nervous when discussing God's sovereignty because of our strong commitment to free-will and human responsibility. Daniel also affirms such commitments, but does so without any qualms about also believing that God is sovereign and orchestrates the developments of history behind the scenes. Many non-biblical apocalyptic writings commend a dualistic worldview in which good and evil duke it out in the end times. Daniel, however, insists that God is sovereign and denies that there can be any true competition since God directs history as the "Most High."

While the Nebuchadnezzars, Belshazzars, and Dariuses of history boast about the might and grandeur of their realms (cf. Daniel 4:30), Daniel insists the God of Israel the directs the play of history in order both to exalt and to humble kings according to His own design, and that is exactly what Nebuchadnezzar was forced to recognize (Daniel 4:34–35).

Although evil and sin remain undeniable realities in the book of Daniel—so much so that an angel was delayed in delivering a messaged to Daniel (Daniel 10:11–13)—the book never suggests there is a meaningful struggle between God and evil. God will guide history to its designed conclusion with the reign of the Son of Man who is worshiped by all the peoples (Daniel 7:13–14).

Responsible Free Will

Given Daniel's insistence on divine sovereignty, it might seem counterintuitive also to claim the book maintains a strong commitment to human responsibility. Contemporary Christians typically stress one or the other of these points. Even so, the Bible—and especially Daniel—rejects any either/or arrangement and insists both that God is sovereign and that humans have free will and are therefore responsible for their actions.

Two examples from the first half of Daniel attest human responsibility. First, in Daniel 1, Daniel and his friends find themselves in exile as a result of God's judgment (Daniel 1:2–3). However, rather than resigning themselves to judgment and embracing sin in exile, Daniel and his compatriots maneuver themselves so that the Babylonian court works around the kosher laws of Leviticus by providing vegetables for food instead of the meat that would be impure in one sense or another. For their efforts, God blessed Daniel and his friends for their responsible faithfulness.

A second example is the experience of Nebuchadnezzar in Daniel 4. Worded as a letter from the king to his subjects, the chapter reports a dream—subsequently interpreted by Daniel—in which Nebuchadnezzar was destined to fall under God's judgment until he became humble before God. While it would seem the hand had been played showing God pre-determined what would happen, Nebuchadnezzar did not experience this judgment until 12 months after the dream when Nebuchadnezzar made the choice to boast about himself in building Babylon "by my mighty power and for the glory of my majesty" (Daniel 4:30). It was at the point of his sinful pride that Nebuchadnezzar experienced God's judgment. God knew the future beforehand and, arguably, the dream was a warning for the king to submit to God. However, like most kings, Nebuchadnezzar was reluctant to submit to a conquered people's deity and so God held him accountable for his behavior.

Optimism for God's People

Daniel's insistence of divine sovereignty and human responsibility mix together to create a final theme for the book: God blesses the faithful. This is an encouraging message for those who have read and continue to read Daniel under the threat of persecution. Sometimes God delivers (Daniel 1:15–17; 3:24–27); sometimes the faithful die (7:25; 11:33–35). Either way, the picture Daniel offers readers is of a God whose hand guides history toward His eternal kingdom in which those who have chosen faithfulness will receive blessing (12:1–3).

As God's people study the book of Daniel today, it is important for us to remember the type of writing that it is and the message that it proclaims: God is leading history to the arrival of His kingdom. As we await that end, we hear the call of Daniel to faithfulness even as kings and nations insist on their own lordship.

---

1. *New Beacon Bible Commentary; Daniel* (Kansas City: Beacon Hill Press of Kansas City, 2009), 193.
2. For more detailed information, consult Jim Edlin, *Daniel*, 37–43.

BEN BOECKEL is an ordained elder who has pastored in Texas and Idaho. He has taught for several Nazarene educational institutions and has published both academic and popular level articles on biblical studies.

SESSION 1

Session Outcome

To learn to develop a trust that God will equip us to live boldly in the midst of a world that opposes God's kingdom.

Customize:

Daniel is the password to access expanded teaching helps on FoundryLeader.com

Discover:

Illustrated Bible Life traces the history of Judaism during the exile, and provides verse-by-verse commentary on the Scripture passage.

Challenges for Faithful Followers

September

1

ENCOUNTERING A HOSTILE CULTURE

God enables His people to live faithfully in a world that opposes His kingdom and seeks to lure them into its values.

THE WORD

DANIEL 1:1-10

In the third year of the reign of Jehoiakim king of Judah, Nebuchadnezzar king of Babylon came to Jerusalem and besieged it. ²And the Lord delivered Jehoiakim king of Judah into his hand, along with some of the articles from the temple of God. These he carried off to the temple of his god in Babylonia and put in the treasure house of his god.

³Then the king ordered Ashpenaz, chief of his court officials, to bring into the king's service some of the Israelites from the royal family and the nobility—⁴young men without any physical defect, handsome, showing aptitude for every kind of learning, well informed, quick to understand, and qualified to serve in the king's palace. He was to teach them the language and literature of the Babylonians. ⁵The king assigned them a daily amount of food and wine from the king's table. They were to be trained for three years, and after that they were to enter the king's service.

⁶Among those who were chosen were some from Judah: Daniel, Hananiah, Mishael and Azariah. ⁷The chief official gave them new names: to Daniel, the name Belteshazzar; to Hananiah, Shadrach; to Mishael, Meshach; and to Azariah, Abednego.

⁸But Daniel resolved not to defile himself with the royal food and wine, and he asked the chief official for permission not to defile himself this way. ⁹Now God had caused the official to show favor and compassion to Daniel, ¹⁰but the official told Daniel, "I am afraid of my lord the king, who has assigned your food and drink. Why should he see you looking worse than the other young men your age? The king would then have my head because of you."

Last Week:

We learned the ways we are to live in expectation for Christ's return.

This Week:

We will learn the ways God gives His followers the strength and guidance to live in a world that opposes kingdom living.

Session 1

17-20

KEY VERSE

¹⁷To these four young men God gave knowledge and understanding of all kinds of literature and learning. And Daniel could understand visions and dreams of all kinds.

¹⁸At the end of the time set by the king to bring them into his service, the chief official presented them to Nebuchadnezzar. ¹⁹The king talked with them, and he found none equal to Daniel, Hananiah, Mishael and Azariah; so they entered the king's service. ²⁰In every matter of wisdom and understanding about which the king questioned them, he found them ten times better than all the magicians and enchanters in his whole kingdom.

ENGAGE THE WORD

THE HOSTILE CULTURE

Daniel 1:1-7

Daniel found himself swept into a hostile world over which he had little control. The powerful Babylonian armies had seized control of the ancient Middle East, including his hometown of Jerusalem in Judah. They took the best and brightest, like Daniel and his friends, to Babylon to be trained to serve the empire. These captives would learn the values and beliefs of the dominant culture by studying "the language and literature of the Babylonians" (v. 4). Such texts included the history and accumulated wisdom of ancient Mesopotamia, going back to the time of the Sumerians.

In every way it seemed that evil prevailed in Daniel's new world. The Babylonians mocked the faith of his family by stripping treasures from the temple in Jerusalem and placing them in a Babylonian temple. This symbolized the triumph of Marduk, the patron god of Babylon, over the God of Israel. The Babylonians intended this to signal that the ancient faith of Israel had become irrelevant. In addition, their captors wined and dined Daniel and his friends with the best food available, the same fare served at "the king's table" (v. 5). They also gave them Babylonian names to indicate assimilation to the new environment. All traces of Israelite culture and faith had seemingly been removed.

September 1, 2024

Watch:

Dr. Jim Edlin introduces this unit on Daniel.

Listen:

FoundryLeader.com: This week's *Illustrated Bible Life* "Article Out Loud" examines how the exile affected the understanding of God held by His people.

Notes:

_____

_____

_____

_____

_____

_____

_____

_____

_____

_____

_____

_____

_____

_____

Did You Know?

The endings of Daniel and his friend's names (-el and -iah) identified them with Israel's God. But the Babylonian names referenced Babylonian gods. Meshach, for example, means "Who is like Aku (the Babylonian moon god)."

THE CULTURE CONFRONTATION

The surrounding culture often seeks to draw us away from our identity in Christ. Jesus knew that His followers must remain in the world, but He told them not to be "of the world" (John 17:15-16). They must live among those who are unfriendly to His kingdom, but not be shaped by them. That is the challenge for every believer in every generation.

Daniel 1:8-10

Though surrounded by ungodly influences, Daniel did not forget his heritage or his faith. In fact, he held more tightly to them in this challenging environment. He "resolved not to defile himself with the royal food and wine" (v. 8). The term "defile" refers to something or someone becoming unfit for God, like a defective sacrifice or immoral person. Daniel felt the royal food would cause him to become unacceptable to God and he decided that could not happen.

Daniel does not explain exactly why the royal food defiled him. It may have been unclean according to Mosaic laws or perhaps offered to Babylonian gods prior to being served at the king's table. Whatever caused the food to defile him does not matter so much. The main point is that he realized it would compromise his relationship with God.

Standing against the current of Babylonian culture would not be easy. It involved considerable risk. He could literally lose his head and cause his superior the same fate. The king might just decide to eliminate them both for going contrary to established protocol. But God provided Daniel opportunity to be faithful: "God caused the official to show favor and sympathy" to him (v. 9). God made a way for Daniel to negotiate an alternative plan that would allow him to maintain his faith. Instead of eating the royal food, Daniel proposed eating only vegetables and drinking water for ten days (v. 12). If his health failed, then the authorities could do with him as they liked. In any case, he would not jeopardize his relationship with God.

 Discover:

Prior to the Babylonian exile, many of God's people believed their nation was invincible. With that mindset, God's people generally ignored the challenging calls to repentance by the prophets. Then God permitted the unthinkable: God allowed the Babylonians to invade and conquer His people. How was this possible? Learn more about how exile matured the faith of God's people in this week's *Illustrated Bible Life* article, "Judaism in Exile."

Think About It

Babylonian literature contained the best collection of human knowledge available in the ancient world. Though mixed with pagan values, it enabled Daniel to understand the dominant culture and know when to challenge it.

THE CULTURE TRANSFORMATION

As the world pushes us toward evil, God opens doors toward good. By God's grace we will find a means to do what is right in the most decadent circumstances. God will "provide a way out so that you can stand" against the temptations of this world (1 Corinthians 10:13).

Daniel 1:17-20

God not only provided a way for Daniel to remain true to his convictions, God also gifted him and his friends with excellent health and superior "knowledge and understanding" (v. 17). After ten days of eating other food, Daniel and his friends "looked healthier and better nourished than any of the young men who ate the royal food" (v. 15). Later, after three years of training, the king examined them and found them "ten times better" than any of the wise men in the kingdom (v. 20). God rewarded the risk these young men took to remain committed to him.

Through this first story, Daniel helps believers see how they can live in the midst of ungodly cultures. At times, Daniel adopted some of the best things from the surrounding culture like its language and literature. He even accepted some of its benign customs such as names that were familiar to his captors.

It is clear, however, that Daniel took a stand when a cultural practice threatened his relationship with God. This confrontation came with considerable risk to himself and those around him. But in the end, God enabled Daniel and his friends to stand firm. As a result, they became transforming agents in the culture.

REFLECT In what ways can you live each day with an "in the world, not of it" mentality?

JIM EDLIN is retired professor of Old Testament at MidAmerica Nazarene University.

Notes:

_____

_____

_____

_____

_____

_____

_____

_____

_____

_____

_____

_____

_____

_____

_____

_____

_____

_____

_____

Discussion Guide

 Connect to My Experience

Think about the last time you were far away from home.

■ Did you get homesick? Why or why not?

■ Have you ever been away from home and experienced loneliness? If so, why?

■ If you were in a foreign country, what changes did you experience? What were all the emotions you felt?

When we travel to new and unfamiliar places we rely on things such as tourist guides, GPS, help from local residents, and so on to help us navigate our new surroundings. During these times, we can often feel lost or helpless. We might find ourselves putting our trust in something or someone to help us get our bearings.

■ During times like these, when is it hardest to trust?

■ What threatens your trust the most? What does it look like to be at our most "empty" and still endure in trusting?

Transition:

Today we begin the story of Daniel and his friends, who were taken with many other Israelites into exile in Babylon. There, Daniel and his friends demonstrate how to trust even when they are in difficult circumstances.

Connect to the Word

Invite someone to read Daniel 1:1-7, then discuss the following,

The story begins with King Nebuchadnezzar of Babylon besieging Jerusalem.

■ From the beginning, how do we know King Nebuchadnezzar acts like he is above God in this story? (He robbed God's temple as if to say that Israel's God and the things in His house "belong" to Babylon and their gods.)

■ Why do you think motivated the king's actions? What kind of significance do you think this could have for these Israelites during their time in exile? (He changed their names in order to honor Babylon's gods instead of God. He attempts to change their identity as followers of God and lead them to become Babylonian in their wisdom and in their faith.)

■ What in the story, so far, might point to the fact that although King Nebuchadnezzar wrongly believes he is above the Lord, God is still greater than him? (The text says that the Lord allowed King Jehoiakim of Judah to fall into his hands, v. 2.)

The king of Babylon brings young Israelite men who are "without any physical defect, handsome, showing aptitude for every kind of learning, well informed, quick to understand, and qualified to serve" (v. 4). He is going to teach them all the wisdom of Babylon. They were to be trained and then enter the king's service. The king even assigned food from his own table.

■ What might make this lifestyle tempting to the Israelites in exile? Do you think it would be difficult to turn down all these benefits without question? Why or why not?

■ What was the king of Babylon attempting to accomplish? (so that they will assimilate into his kingdom)

■ In what ways does the world try to squeeze believers into its mold?

Invite someone to read Daniel 1:8-10, then discuss the following,

Daniel would not eat the royal food and his friends appear to have followed suit.

- Why did Daniel turn down the food and wine from the king's table? What is it about the things offered by the king that might "defile" Daniel? (The exact reasons are unclear; however, whatever the reasons, Daniel felt that partaking in those things were incompatible with His relationship with God.)

- Do you think this was a difficult decision for Daniel? If so, why? What would have made this a hard thing to refuse?

The official feared that Daniel and his friends would start to look malnourished. If they fail, it is his head and theirs. But Daniel requested that they feed them vegetables to eat and water to drink for ten days. After that, compare their appearance with those who ate the royal food (w. 12-14).

- How did Daniel's actions run counter to the conventional wisdom of the day?

Invite someone to read Daniel 1:17-20, then discuss the following,

After ten days of refusing the king's food and wine, the opposite of the official's expectations happened: Daniel and his friends were more well-nourished than their counterparts! The king found none equal to these four.

- In what ways was Daniel's diet more than just about healthy eating habits?

- Why is it that Daniel and his friends succeed? (They trusted God, who gave them knowledge and understanding.)

- What does God's work in this situation tell us about the God of Israel?

Connect to My Life and the World

Daniel does not refuse to learn the wisdom of the Babylonians; however, he stays faithful to God.

- What does this tell us about learning from others with whom we disagree? (It is not a sin to seek understanding even from those we disagree with, but to surrender our identity in order to do so is sinful. We are to engage prayerfully and carefully as we learn.)

Daniel stays faithful to his identity as a follower of God by refusing the king's food.

- What are the things which our culture sees as normal and necessary that would hurt our relationship with God if we indulged in them? What are the lines that we should not cross in order to stay faithful to our identity in Christ?

- How do we discern what is faithful to our identity as followers of Jesus even as we engage with our neighbors who do not always believe as we do?

- What keeps us grounded in the truth? How does God teach us what is good and what is to be avoided?

- What does it look like to depend on God when we have to give up what might look good on the surface, but is not pleasing to the Lord?

Close in prayer.

Sessions 1-7 are written by Austin Troyer

Austin is the pastor of the Church of the Nazarene in Tahlequah, OK, having served there for 8 years. He also serves as an adjunct professor at Northwest Nazarene University.

Challenges for Faithful Followers

SESSION 2

Session Outcome

To help people explore the meaning of revelation and interpretation, and how both are relevant to daily living in God's wisdom.

Customize:

Daniel is the password to access expanded teaching helps on FoundryLeader.com

 **Discover:**

Illustrated Bible Life examines the role of wisdom in biblical literature, and provides verse-by-verse commentary on the Scripture passage.

September

8

SEEKING WISDOM FOR LIFE

Only God can give us the true wisdom we need for living today and into the future.

THE WORD

DANIEL 2:1-11

In the second year of his reign, Nebuchadnezzar had dreams; his mind was troubled and he could not sleep. ²So the king summoned the magicians, enchanters, sorcerers and astrologers to tell him what he had dreamed. When they came in and stood before the king, ³he said to them, "I have had a dream that troubles me and I want to know what it means."

⁴Then the astrologers answered the king, "May the king live forever! Tell your servants the dream, and we will interpret it."

⁵The king replied to the astrologers, "This is what I have firmly decided: If you do not tell me what my dream was and interpret it, I will have you cut into pieces and your houses turned into piles of rubble. ⁶But if you tell me the dream and explain it, you will receive from me gifts and rewards and great honor. So tell me the dream and interpret it for me."

⁷Once more they replied, "Let the king tell his servants the dream, and we will interpret it."

⁸Then the king answered, "I am certain that you are trying to gain time, because you realize that this is what I have firmly decided: ⁹If you do not tell me the dream, there is only one penalty for you. You have conspired to tell me misleading and wicked things, hoping the situation will change. So then, tell me the dream, and I will know that you can interpret it for me."

¹⁰The astrologers answered the king, "There is no one on earth who can do what the king asks! No king, however great and mighty, has ever asked such a thing of any magician or enchanter or astrol-

Last Week:

We discovered that, by God's grace, we can stand against the pressures of a dominant, worldly, culture.

This Week:

We will discover how God alone possesses the true wisdom we need for today and tomorrow.

Session 2

oger. ¹¹What the king asks is too difficult. No one can reveal it to the king except the gods, and they do not live among humans."

17-28a

¹⁷Then Daniel returned to his house and explained the matter to his friends Hananiah, Mishael and Azariah. ¹⁸He urged them to plead for mercy from the God of heaven concerning this mystery, so that he and his friends might not be executed with the rest of the wise men of Babylon. ¹⁹During the night the mystery was revealed to Daniel in a vision. Then Daniel praised the God of heaven ²⁰and said: **"Praise be to the name of God for ever and ever; wisdom and power are his.**

KEY VERSES

²¹He changes times and seasons; he deposes kings and raises up others. He gives wisdom to the wise and knowledge to the discerning.

²²He reveals deep and hidden things; he knows what lies in darkness, and light dwells with him.

²³I thank and praise you, God of my ancestors: You have given me wisdom and power, you have made known to me what we asked of you, you have made known to us the dream of the king."

²⁴Then Daniel went to Arioch, whom the king had appointed to execute the wise men of Babylon, and said to him, "Do not execute the wise men of Babylon. Take me to the king, and I will interpret his dream for him."

²⁵Arioch took Daniel to the king at once and said, "I have found a man among the exiles from Judah who can tell the king what his dream means."

²⁶The king asked Daniel (also called Belteshazzar), "Are you able to tell me what I saw in my dream and interpret it?"

²⁷Daniel replied, "No wise man, enchanter, magician or diviner can explain to the king the mystery he has asked about, ²⁸but there is a God in heaven who reveals mysteries. He has shown King Nebuchadnezzar what will happen in days to come.

ENGAGE THE WORD

A KING NEEDS WISDOM

Daniel 2:1-11

King Nebuchadnezzar needed wisdom to interpret a dream. He had dreamed something that did not make sense and deeply troubled him. Like many people in the ancient world, the king believed the gods communicated with people through dreams. He also

Listen:

FoundryLeader.com: What is biblical wisdom? We'll look at this question and others in this week's *Illustrated Bible Life* "Article Out Loud."

Notes:

_____

_____

_____

_____

_____

_____

_____

_____

_____

_____

_____

_____

_____

_____

_____

_____

_____

Did You Know?
Biblical wisdom includes understanding how the world works and where life choices may take us. Knowing this enables a person to do the right thing at the right time in the right way.

knew that such dreams frequently carried foreboding messages.

So, Nebuchadnezzar called upon his most skilled interpreters, "the magicians, enchanters, sorcerers and astrologers" (v. 2). Each of these possessed particular abilities deemed useful for decoding communication from the divine realm. Some of them had studied records of past dreams. Others analyzed animal entrails or relied on ecstatic experiences to gain insight. Still others studied the movement of stars for clues. Once these experts determined the heavenly message, they devised incantations and potions to ward off its evil effects.

Normally, Babylonian wise men began with the content of a dream. Then they could suggest possible interpretations as well as remedies for its consequences. But Nebuchadnezzar refused to tell his wise men what was in the dream. He thought they should be able to do that.

Nebuchadnezzar expected far too much from human wisdom. The Babylonian wise men cconfessed: "There is no one on earth who can do what the king asks ... no one can reveal it to the king except the gods" (vv. 10-11). Even they knew only the divine could interpret the dream.

GOD REVEALS WISDOM

Daniel 2:17-23

Daniel's answer to finding wisdom was to turn to God. So, Daniel and his friends prayed earnestly for God to reveal the meaning of "this mystery" (v. 18). The word "mystery" refers to something that is secret or unknown to humans. By calling the dream a mystery they affirmed the same thing that their Babylonian colleagues had confessed. Their understanding was not adequate. They needed insight only God could provide.

Daniel understood that if God revealed the meaning of this mystery it would be because of God's "mercy" (v. 18). He knew that God is under no obligation to

 **Discover:**

What is biblical wisdom? To put it simply, biblical wisdom is skill for living life well. That means living in harmony with the order of the universe that God created. As a result, a wise person does the right thing at the right time in the right way. Let's look deeper into what this means for Christian living in this week's *Illustrated Bible Life* article, "What Is Biblical Wisdom?"

Notes:

Session 2

Think About It

Even though God revealed the meaning of the king's dream to Daniel, people have continued to debate its details for centuries. Its main message remains clear, however: God overrules the rulers of this world.

DANIEL SHARES WISDOM

share divine insight with humans. When He does, it is neither expected nor merited. God reveals wisdom out of the goodness of His heart.

Somewhere in the night, God "made known" to Daniel what the king had dreamed and what it meant (v. 23). In response, Daniel sang a song of praise that honored God for giving "wisdom to the wise" (v. 21). According to Proverbs 9:10, "the wise" are those who fear the Lord, like Daniel and his friends. They look to God for understanding and insight because true wisdom resides with God alone.

Daniel 2:24-28a

When Daniel stood before King Nebuchadnezzar, he affirmed once more what Babylon's wise men had confessed. He could not know the meaning of the king's dream using his own skills. He admitted, "No wise man ... can explain to the king the mystery" (v. 27). However, he went on to say, "There is a God in heaven who reveals mysteries" (v. 28). God knows what humans do not know and chooses to share it as He wills.

Daniel explained the king's dream because God graciously revealed it to him. The dream was about an enormous statue of precious metals being crushed by a rock. Its images were stunning as well as puzzling. Its message, however, was not complicated. Simply put, the dream proclaimed that though earthly kingdoms appear impressive and strong, God's kingdom overcomes them all. Such truth is wisdom for life in any generation. It encourages people who belong to God and warns those who do not. God's people can be courageous and remain steadfast, because God wins in the end.

REFLECT In what ways do you need God's wisdom today?

JIM EDLIN

Discussion Guide

Connect to My Experience

Begin your session by asking,

■ What do you do when you do not know something? How do you know what a good source of information is?

Even with so much information at our fingertips, there is still so much that is hard to figure out. Trying to understand and not being able to come up with the answers can cause us to worry or even fear.

■ When have you felt anxious because of something that you did not understand or a problem you could not figure out?

■ How do we see people in our world typically react to their lack of understanding?

■ How do you usually react when you cannot find the answer you are looking for? Who do you go to for wisdom? How do you know who is wise?

Transition:

It is important to know a reliable source of wisdom. Daniel responds to a deeply troubled king who is seeking wisdom in the wrong ways and from the wrong sources.

Connect to the Word

Invite someone to read Daniel 2:1-11, then discuss the following,

The king of Babylon begins to have troubling dreams he does not understand.

■ What can we learn from the way he reacts to his anxiety and lack of understanding?

At first, the wise people of the kingdom are confident that they can interpret the dream. But the king demands that they give an interpretation without even hearing him describe the dream first!

■ Why do you think the king makes this impossible demand? (He is seeking real answers.)

■ How does the confidence of the magicians, enchanters, sorcerers, and astrologers change after they hear the king's demands?

The astrologers respond to the king's request: "There is no one on earth who can do what the king asks!" (v. 10).

■ What can we learn from their response?

■ How might we be tempted to respond in the same way when we are facing a seemingly impossible situation?

Invite someone to read Daniel 2:17-23, then discuss the following,

Wisely, Daniel does not panic, but begins to ask questions to seek the source of the problem. When he hears why the king is upset, he asks for more time. But Daniel cannot do this alone!

■ What does Daniel do in response to the limits of his own understanding? (He brings the problem to his friends so that they can pray for God's help together.)

God reveals the meaning of the dream to Daniel.

■ How does Daniel respond to God making known the meaning of the dream?

■ Why is it appropriate for Daniel to praise God in this moment?

■ What are some things that Daniel mentions in his hymn of praise that testify

Insight

The way that God works to provide strength, wisdom, and faith to Daniel and his friends leads the kings of Babylon to testify about the greatness of God. God is alive, active, and being made known even in this place far from the temple in Jerusalem.

to God's wisdom and understanding? How does it acknowledge that God's wisdom is higher than ours?

- Why does Daniel describe God's revealing the meaning of the dream as "mercy" (v. 18)? (God does not have to do this. This action is not earned, but God graciously hears Daniel's prayer and answers.)

- What about the king's struggle demonstrates the lack of power and mercy of his "gods"? (It is Daniel's God that both knows the dream and gives understanding.)

Invite someone to read Daniel 2:24-28a, then discuss the following,

Daniel tells Arioch, the king's executioner, to not kill the wise men of Babylon. He will interpret the king's dream. Daniel, rather keeping silent and having these men seemingly get what was coming to them, he advocated for mercy be shown to these men.

- Do you think that it is significant or surprising that Daniel specifically asks for the Babylonian wise men to be spared? If so, why?

- Why is it important for us to desire (or show) mercy to be shown to others? (Daniel sought God's mercy, and in turn, understood that followers of God must show mercy to others.)

The king asks Daniel directly if he can do what he has asked; that is, tell the king his own dream and interpret what it means.

- What can we learn from Daniel's response? (He agrees with Babylon's wise men that no one can do this, except for God!)

Daniel then tells the king what God has revealed to him, the dream and its interpretation.

- In what ways doe this point to God's wisdom and understanding being greater than what all of the earthly kingdoms can gather together?

Connect to My Life and the World

Nebuchadnezzar asks his wise men and Daniel to do the impossible—read his mind about what is troubling him and give him advice.

- Has someone brought a question or situation to you for prayer or advice? If so, how did you respond?

- Is the church a safe place to bring our questions and lack of understanding? If not, why should we aim for the church to become a safe place?

Daniel, who could not interpret the dream on his own, shows us that the best place to take our lack of wisdom is to the God of all understanding.

- How does God respond to our lack of wisdom and understanding? Can we bring those things to God? If so, why do you think we are able to do so?

- What resources does God give us to help guide us into wisdom and deeper faith?

- How should we respond when God does not give us the full answer?

- How should we respond when God answers our prayer and guides us in understanding?

Close in prayer.

Unit 1

Challenges for Faithful Followers

Session Outcome

To understand the ways that God provides us with the power and strength to serve Him.

Customize:

Daniel is the password to access expanded teaching helps on FoundryLeader.com

Discover:

Who was the fourth person in the fiery furnace with Daniel's friends? *Illustrated Bible Life* looks at this question, and provides verse-by-verse commentary on the Scripture passage.

September

15

LIVING IN THE FIRE

When circumstances are against us, the Lord stands beside us.

THE WORD

DANIEL 3:8-20

At this time some astrologers came forward and denounced the Jews. ⁹They said to King Nebuchadnezzar, "May the king live forever! ¹⁰Your Majesty has issued a decree that everyone who hears the sound of the horn, flute, zither, lyre, harp, pipe and all kinds of music must fall down and worship the image of gold, ¹¹and that whoever does not fall down and worship will be thrown into a blazing furnace. ¹²But there are some Jews whom you have set over the affairs of the province of Babylon—Shadrach, Meshach and Abednego—who pay no attention to you, Your Majesty. They neither serve your gods nor worship the image of gold you have set up."

¹³Furious with rage, Nebuchadnezzar summoned Shadrach, Meshach and Abednego. So these men were brought before the king, ¹⁴and Nebuchadnezzar said to them, "Is it true, Shadrach, Meshach and Abednego, that you do not serve my gods or worship the image of gold I have set up? ¹⁵Now when you hear the sound of the horn, flute, zither, lyre, harp, pipe and all kinds of music, if you are ready to fall down and worship the image I made, very good. But if you do not worship it, you will be thrown immediately into a blazing furnace. Then what god will be able to rescue you from my hand?"

¹⁶Shadrach, Meshach and Abednego replied to him, "King Nebuchadnezzar, we do not need to defend ourselves before you in this matter. **KEY VERSES** ¹⁷If we are thrown into the blazing furnace, the God we serve is able to deliver us from it, and he will deliver us from Your Majesty's hand. ¹⁸But even if he does not, we want you to know, Your Majesty, that we will not serve your gods or worship the image of gold you have set up."

Last Week:

We examined how we must seek godly wisdom for our lives today and for the future.

This Week:

We will examine the ways, by God's grace and by the power of His presence, we can stand against the crowd when we stand for the Lord.

Session 3

¹⁹Then Nebuchadnezzar was furious with Shadrach, Meshach and Abednego, and his attitude toward them changed. He ordered the furnace heated seven times hotter than usual ²⁰and commanded some of the strongest soldiers in his army to tie up Shadrach, Meshach and Abednego and throw them into the blazing furnace.

24-26

²⁴Then King Nebuchadnezzar leaped to his feet in amazement and asked his advisers, "Weren't there three men that we tied up and threw into the fire?"

They replied, "Certainly, Your Majesty."

²⁵He said, "Look! I see four men walking around in the fire, unbound and unharmed, and the fourth looks like a son of the gods."

²⁶Nebuchadnezzar then approached the opening of the blazing furnace and shouted, "Shadrach, Meshach and Abednego, servants of the Most High God, come out! Come here!"

So Shadrach, Meshach and Abednego came out of the fire.

ENGAGE THE WORD

THE DILEMMA

Daniel 3:8-15

King Nebuchadnezzar did not learn much from his dream in chapter 2. He continued to imagine that he ruled the world rather than God. As a result, he set up an impressive golden image and invited everyone in his kingdom to its dedication. Whether the image was a likeness of himself, one of his gods, or something else, we are not told. In any case, it represented his grandeur and might.

At the dedication ceremony, Nebuchadnezzar offered two options to his subjects: bow or burn. He decreed that everyone must "fall down and worship the image of gold" when music played (v. 9). Anyone who did not bow down would be "thrown into a blazing furnace" (v. 11). This decree included everyone, all "peoples, nations and men of every language" according to verse 4. No one was excluded.

"Some astrologers" (v. 8) revealed their prejudice and jealousy when they reported Shadrach, Meshach, and Abednego to the king. They describe their co-workers as "Jews whom you have set over the affairs

🔊 **Listen:**

FoundryLeader.com: The fourth person in the fiery furnace with Shadrach, Meshach, and Abednego is the focus of this week's *Illustrated Bible Life* "Article Out Loud."

Notes:

_____

_____

_____

_____

_____

_____

_____

_____

_____

_____

_____

_____

_____

_____

_____

_____

_____

Did You Know?
Today's story contains humor in the way it mocks Babylonian worship. The long list of musical instruments ridicules the futility of pompous worship designed to get the attention of preoccupied, unsympathetic gods of Babylon.

THE DECISION

of the province of Babylon" (v. 12). They might have added, "instead of us." Those foreigners had the jobs that they wanted.

When Nebuchadnezzar learned of the stance that Shadrach, Meshach, and Abednego had taken, he became "furious with rage" (v. 13). He apparently felt disrespected. Godly people often upset arrogant people of this world. So, when the king pronounced his ultimatum once again, he finished with a taunt. He mockingly asked, "Then what god will be able to rescue you from my hand?" (v. 15).

Daniel 3:16-20

Though Nebuchadnezzar may have intended his question as rhetorical, Shadrach, Meshach, and Abednego responded as if he had asked for an answer. They declared, "the God we serve is able to save us" and "will rescue us from your hand" (v. 17). They believed God fully capable of overcoming any threat that this world might throw at them. But they left the outcome in God's hands. They did not presume to tell God what to do. If God chose not to rescue them, they would still hold fast to their convictions. They would not break God's commandments and "serve your gods" or "worship the image of gold" (v. 18). God had put these laws first in the list of Ten Commandments for a reason. That is where a committed relationship to God begins.

Shadrach, Meshach, and Abednego firmly decided to go with God rather than the crowd. Intimidation from peers and the most powerful man in the world did not alter their decision. There was no room for discussion. They did "not need to defend" their actions, because they were guilty as charged (v. 16). They had chosen God's way, not the way of the world.

Such conviction is very admirable. But it does not always gain the respect of the world. In the case of Shadrach, Meshach, and Abednego, it intensified the fury of the king and the heat of the furnace at the

Discover:

Interpreters have long been interested in understanding who was the fourth person in the fiery furnace with Shadrach, Meshach, and Abednego in Daniel 3:24-25. The history of interpretation of Daniel 3 offers us several interesting insights about how rabbinic and Christian scholars have interpreted the book of Daniel. This week's *Illustrated Bible Life* article examines the identity of "The Fourth Person."

Notes:

Session 3

Think About It

Nebuchadnezzar constructed an idol to promote himself. But in the end, this provided a means to display God's greatness. We might wonder what other means God could use to reveal himself in this world.

THE DELIVERANCE

same time. In the end, their faith in God got them thrown into the fire.

Daniel 3:24-26

God may not have rescued his servants from being thrown into the fire. But He did protect them in the midst of it and eventually delivered them from it. Nebuchadnezzar and his advisers witnessed this first-hand. They saw the three Jewish men "walking around in the fire, unbound and unharmed" (v. 25). This is remarkable since the soldiers who carried out the execution died from the heat. Surviving the furnace was impossible. But God overcame the impossible.

Further, the king observed another person with them who looked "like a son of the gods" (v. 25). Whether this was an angel, as the king noted later in verse 28, or perhaps even Jesus before His birth, we cannot say for certain. What remains important is that God came alongside His committed servants in their distress. God went with His faithful followers into the fire. Those who stood up for God did not stand alone.

In the end, the king who ordered the execution reversed it. He invited Shadrach, Meshach, and Abednego to "come out" of the furnace (v. 26). Then, he acknowledged that the God of these men must be "the Most High God" (v. 26). For Nebuchadnezzar, this meant that the Jewish God headed up the pantheon of gods in his world. He was partly right. Though there is no collection of other gods, the God of Shadrach, Meshach, and Abednego is greater than any divine power one might imagine. This God goes into the furnace with those who chose to go against the crowd and stand for Him.

REFLECT Is there a fiery situation from which you need God's rescue?

JIM EDLIN

Discussion Guide

 Connect to My Experience

When we have deep passions, it becomes an important part of our conversations, habits, and even personalities.

- ■ What is something you are passionate about? How did you develop this passion?
- ■ What do you do or say that shows that part of your interests?
- ■ In what ways do our passions effect our actions?

Transition:

Throughout Daniel, we are reminded that there are things that threaten our faith in God, passions that do not mix with righteousness. Today, we will see that faith in God is something worth living for no matter what.

 **Connect to the Word**

Invite someone to read Daniel 3:8-15, then discuss the following,

King Nebuchadnezzar's decree that everyone bow to the statue he had built came with a warning. If people did not bow, they would be thrown into the fiery furnace.

- ■ Why do you think that the king made this decree? What is the purpose behind the statue and the punishment? Why was everyone required to obey?
- ■ What do you think motivated people to obey this command?

Some in the crowd of people who bowed could not help but notice that Shadrach, Meshach, and Abednego did not bow to the king's statue.

- ■ What do you think motivated the people who turned in Shadrach, Meshach, and Abednego? How do people react today toward Christians who refuse to bow to worldly idols?

The king sends for them and asks them to confess to the claims that they will not bow. He gives them the option to bow when the call comes again.

- ■ Why do you think that the king gives them this second chance? (The king is confident in his fire, claiming that no god will be able to save them.)

Invite someone to read Daniel 3:16-20, then discuss the following,

The king has just laid out the dire consequences if they do not obey and bow. Shadrach, Meshach, and Abednego respond to the king, "We do not need to defend ourselves before you in this matter."

- ■ Why do they not seem to be threatened by the punishment of the king?
- ■ Faced with an enraged King Nebuchadnezzar and the condemnation from others who brought this news to the king, what kind of pressure do you think that these three faced?
- ■ The king asks, "What god will be able to rescue you from my hand?" Where had Shadrach, Meshach, and Abednego already determined to place their trust for deliverance?

The friends continue, "But even if he does not...we will not serve your gods or worship the image of gold you have set up."

- ■ What do you think they mean by this statement? How does this demonstrate their faith in God? What do you think it takes for them to say this to the king?

The king is so furious he turns up the heat and has them tied up and thrown into the furnace.

Insight

Though it is unclear exactly what he saw, Nebuchadnezzar's description of the fourth figure in the furnace was as one "like a son of the gods." He most likely thought that a deity was present with them. The king's declaration points out that "Shadrach, Meshach, and Abednego were not delivered from the fire. They were delivered in the midst of the fire."[1]

Invite someone to read Daniel 3:24-26, then discuss the following,

- Have you ever been in a situation that seemed seven times hotter than normal and it felt like your hands were tied? If so, what did you learn from that experience?

Shadrach, Meshach, and Abednego are now in the fiery furnace. It might have seemed to others that God had not delivered them like they said was possible. But the three survive the fire.

- What in this scene might make those watching think there was no hope for these three?

- Are we ever short-sighted when it comes to being hopeful for the spiritual rescue of those who seem to be in a seemingly hopeless situation?

The king is astonished at what he sees in the fire. He even sees a fourth figure alongside these three in the fire.

- While we do not know the exact nature of this presence the king saw, how does it show that our God, the true God, walks with the persecuted and is able to deliver us from evil and dire circumstances?

- Why does Nebuchadnezzar's opinion change about the God of Shadrach, Meshach, and Abednego?

- Do you think king Nebuchadnezzar is still lacking in his understanding of the Lord? Why or why not? (He says he is the "Most High God" as if to say that God is the one with the highest rank. But we know that God is the only one to be worshiped. All others who claim to be gods, including the king and his statue, are false.)

Connect to My Life and the World

Just when it seemed like there was no hope, Shadrach, Meshach, and Abednego were saved from the fire and God stood with them.

- Have you experienced God's presence and protection in a surprising or amazing way? If so, how?

- In what ways has God delivered you from evils like the fiery furnace or the king of Babylon?

- What does it take for us to develop an unconditional trust in God like Shadrach, Meshach, and Abednego?

God helps us to stand against the idols of this world. More than that, God also helps us to act in ways that show our dedication to Him.

- How do we discern what the idols are in the world?

- What are the things that we do that say "we will not bow" to those idols? How do our deeds testify to what God we serve?

- What are some of the things that Christians should be standing for no matter what comes their way?

- What would it look like for us to be dedicated to God's ways here in our community?

Close in prayer.

---

1. Jim Edlin, *NBBC: Daniel* (Kansas City; Beacon Hill Press of Kansas City, 2009), 99.

SESSION 4

Session Outcome

To recognize that the sin of arrogance is a sin against God and others.

Customize:

Daniel is the password to access expanded teaching helps on FoundryLeader.com

🔍 **Discover:**

Illustrated Bible Life examines the meaning of the Babylonian words mene, tekel, and parsin, and provides verse-by-verse commentary on the Scripture passage.

Challenges for Faithful Followers

September

22

THE SIN OF ARROGANCE

God holds people accountable for their arrogance.

THE WORD

DANIEL 5:1-5

King Belshazzar gave a great banquet for a thousand of his nobles and drank wine with them. ²While Belshazzar was drinking his wine, he gave orders to bring in the gold and silver goblets that Nebuchadnezzar his father had taken from the temple in Jerusalem, so that the king and his nobles, his wives and his concubines might drink from them. ³So they brought in the gold goblets that had been taken from the temple of God in Jerusalem, and the king and his nobles, his wives and his concubines drank from them. ⁴As they drank the wine, they praised the gods of gold and silver, of bronze, iron, wood and stone.

⁵Suddenly the fingers of a human hand appeared and wrote on the plaster of the wall, near the lampstand in the royal palace. The king watched the hand as it wrote.

8-9

⁸Then all the king's wise men came in, but they could not read the writing or tell the king what it meant. ⁹So King Belshazzar became even more terrified and his face grew more pale. His nobles were baffled.

17-30

¹⁷Then Daniel answered the king, "You may keep your gifts for yourself and give your rewards to someone else. Nevertheless, I will read the writing for the king and tell him what it means.

¹⁸"Your Majesty, the Most High God gave your father Nebuchadnezzar sovereignty and greatness and glory and splendor. ¹⁹Because of the high position he gave him, all the nations and peoples of every language dreaded and feared him. Those the king wanted to put to death, he put to death; those he wanted to spare, he spared; those he wanted to promote,

Last Week:

We saw that those who stand up for God will never stand alone because His presence is always with us.

This Week:

We will see how God holds people accountable for their arrogant attitudes and actions.

he promoted; and those he wanted to humble, he humbled. ²⁰But when his heart became arrogant and hardened with pride, he was deposed from his royal throne and stripped of his glory. ²¹He was driven away from people and given the mind of an animal; he lived with the wild donkeys and ate grass like the ox; and his body was drenched with the dew of heaven, until he acknowledged that the Most High God is sovereign over all kingdoms on earth and sets over them anyone he wishes.

KEY VERSES

²²"But you, Belshazzar, his son, have not humbled yourself, though you knew all this. ²³Instead, you have set yourself up against the Lord of heaven. You had the goblets from his temple brought to you, and you and your nobles, your wives and your concubines drank wine from them. You praised the gods of silver and gold, of bronze, iron, wood and stone, which cannot see or hear or understand. But you did not honor the God who holds in his hand your life and all your ways. ²⁴Therefore he sent the hand that wrote the inscription.

²⁵"This is the inscription that was written: mene, mene, tekel, parsin

²⁶"Here is what these words mean: Mene: God has numbered the days of your reign and brought it to an end.

²⁷Tekel: You have been weighed on the scales and found wanting.

²⁸Peres: Your kingdom is divided and given to the Medes and Persians."

²⁹Then at Belshazzar's command, Daniel was clothed in purple, a gold chain was placed around his neck, and he was proclaimed the third highest ruler in the kingdom.

³⁰That very night Belshazzar, king of the Babylonians, was slain.

ENGAGE THE WORD

ARROGANCE DISPLAYED

Daniel 5:1-4

Belshazzar wanted to impress the leaders of his realm. So, he put on a great banquet, surrounded himself with thousands of the nation's leading citizens, and let wine flow freely. All this likely took place in the massive throne room hall of "the royal palace" complex in Babylon (v. 5).

In order to accentuate his importance further, Belshazzar ordered "gold and silver goblets" be used for drinking wine (v. 2). These were no ordinary goblets however. They came from the plunder of the

🔊 **Listen:**

FoundryLeader.com: What was the meaning of the writing on the wall during Belshazzar's feast in Daniel 5? This week's *Illustrated Bible Life* "Article Out Loud" explains.

Notes:

_____

_____

_____

_____

_____

_____

_____

_____

_____

_____

_____

_____

_____

_____

_____

_____

_____

Did You Know?
Babylonian records never officially designated Belshazzar as king. His father, Nabonidus, was the ruling monarch and only placed his son in authority during his absence from the city of Babylon.

Jewish temple in Jerusalem during the days of his predecessor Nebuchadnezzar. Drinking from them not only underscored the dominating reach of Babylonian empire, it also expressed contempt for the God of the Jews. Belshazzar flaunted a fearless disregard for God. To push the point further, he used the goblets to toast the images of gods collected from other conquests. Ironically, some of these idols were made of the same material as the goblets.

By the world's standards, Belshazzar appeared to have much to boast about. He seemed to wield great power, possess vast resources, and attract many friends. In addition, he showed no fear of offending the divine realms. All of this, however, was misplaced pride of a petty person.

ARROGANCE CHALLENGED

Daniel 5:5, 8-9

God disrupted Belshazzar's self-promoting party in a startling manner. A disembodied "human hand appeared and wrote on the plaster of the wall" (v. 5). Such a sight captured everyone's attention, especially the king's. His brazen arrogance quickly disappeared and his pretentious shell of confidence dissolved. The entire banquet had been a show and Belshazzar knew it. According to ancient historians, he likely knew that Persian armies were within a few miles of Babylon. They had captured key cities and were marching toward the capitol to complete the conquest.

Knowing this made the message on the wall all the more unsettling to the king. Yet, none of his wise men could read it let alone "tell the king what it meant" (v. 8). Babylon's best diviners failed to understand what God was saying. They were skilled in hearing other voices, but not God's. The words of God made no sense to those unaccustomed to hearing Him speak.

ARROGANCE EXPOSED

Daniel 5:17-30

Belshazzar's only hope of understanding God's words to him came through a man who was in touch

Discover:

The Babylonian ruler Belshazzar held a feast during which he called for some of the treasures of the Jerusalem temple. Such a blasphemous use of sacred objects called down God's wrath, and a disembodied hand wrote a mysterious message on the wall of the palace. What was the meaning of this foreboding message? Find out in this week's *Illustrated Bible Life* article, "Mene, Mene, Tekel, Parsin."

Session 4

Think About It

In the end, both Daniel and Belshazzar received their just rewards. Daniel was promoted for his humility and wisdom, while Belshazzar was demoted for his arrogance and ignorance.

with God, Daniel. The message, as the king suspected, was not encouraging.

Before interpreting the wall writing though, Daniel began with a history lesson. He recapped the story recorded in Daniel 4 about Belshazzar's most famous predecessor Nebuchadnezzar. He had flaunted his power too. But God humbled him "until he acknowledged that the Most High God is sovereign" (5:21). This highlighted a crucial difference between the two kings. Nebuchadnezzar eventually submitted to the authority of God, but Belshazzar had "not humbled" himself (v. 22). In an effort to impress people Belshazzar had set himself "up against the Lord of heaven" (v. 23).

Belshazzar acted as if he answered to no one. But, in fact, he did. Daniel told him that the God he refused to honor actually "holds in his hands your life" (v. 23). The king of Babylon was accountable to One greater than himself. God would assess his life and administer justice. This was the message of the four words on the wall. Belshazzar's actions and attitudes had been "weighed" *(Tekel)* on God's scales of justice and not measured up (v. 27). Therefore, God had "numbered" *(Mene)* the days that the king would reign (5:26). He would sit on the throne only as long as God decided. Then, the Babylonian kingdom would come to an end. It would be "divided" *(Peres)* and conquered by their enemies the Medes and the Persians (5:28).

God's message found immediate fulfillment as "that very night Belshazzar...was slain and Darius the Mede took over the kingdom" (5:30). The trap of arrogance snared another pompous pretender, while God continued to rule over heaven and earth.

REFLECT Pray, asking God to show you any areas of your life where arrogant attitudes might have crept in?

JIM EDLIN

Discussion Guide

Connect to My Experience

Silently consider what comes to mind when you hear the word "pride."

■ Is it okay to be proud? If so, about what should we be proud? Can pride get out of hand?

Proverbs 16:18 says, "Pride goes before destruction, a haughty spirit before a fall."

■ What is your reaction to this passage? Do you find it to be true? What is pride and why does it often lead to the downfall of the proud? Do the proud always fall?

Pride can set us up for being humbled; brought down from our "high horse" so to speak.

■ What is a humbling experience you have gone through? What did it feel like to be humbled? Do you think that you needed that experience?

■ Why is humility a good thing? How does being humble balance out our pride?

Transition:

The new king of Babylon, Belshazzar, is arrogant and thinks highly of himself and his power. In today's passage, the God who exalts the humble and humbles the proud responds to the pride of this king.

Connect to the Word

Invite someone to read Daniel 5:1-4, then discuss the following,

Belshazzar calls the assembly of his wives and nobility to drink from cups stolen from the temple. He asserts himself above the gods of the other nations, including the God of Israel.

■ What message does this assembly send? (Consider how it might establish Belshazzar as king and celebrate his wealth and power.)

■ In what ways do people demonstrate irreverence toward the things of God today?

They praise their gods, "the gods of gold and silver, of bronze, iron, wood and stone" (v. 4).

■ What makes these gods they worship different from the God of Israel?

■ In what ways have you seen people praise the gods of "gold and silver, of bronze, iron, wood and stone" today?

Invite someone to read Daniel 5:5, 8-9, then discuss the following,

Suddenly, what looks like a hand begins to write on the wall. Mesmerized, the king's "face turned pale and he was so frightened that his legs became weak and his knees were knocking" (v. 6).

■ How would you have responded to this if you were in that room?

■ Why do you think it is significant that God responds to the king's arrogant display?

Just like when Nebuchadnezzar had a dream he did not understand, Belshazzar calls all of his wise men to seek understanding.

■ What do you notice about the way the king and nobility respond as more and more wise men fail to come up with an answer about what has happened?

■ How might this remind us of the previous king of Babylon's actions when he could not understand?

Invite someone to read Daniel 5:17-30, then discuss the following,

In the middle of the confusion, the queen remembers Daniel (vv. 10-11). Belshazzar sends for him and offers a handsome reward if Daniel were to interpret the writing.

Insight

The people of Babylon constantly greet their king with the phrase, "O king, live forever." Yet, even as Daniel still lives, a few of Babylon's kings die. It is only the King of Kings who lives forever and gives everlasting life; whose kingdom is eternal.

- How does Daniel respond to the offer? Why do you think that Daniel refused the gifts of the king?

- How does Daniel's rejection of the things that the king offers display the consistency of his character?

Daniel points out the arrogance of the Babylonian kings.

- What does Daniel say happened to Nebuchadnezzar when he did not humble himself before the Lord?

After pointing Nebuchadnezzar's tragic fate, he says, "But you, Belshazzar, his son, have not humbled yourself, though you knew all this" (v. 22).

- What truth is Daniel pointing out to the king, and to us today?

- In what ways is the saying "Those who forget the past are condemned to repeat it" applicable to this story?

- What does it mean that "God holds in his hand your life and all your ways"?

- How would you summarize the interpretation that Daniel offers to the king about these words?

- How does God bring fulfillment to the words written on the wall?

- What message does this send to leaders like Belshazzar and to the rest of the Babylonian people? (God still reigns and will honor the humble and humble the proud.)

Connect to My Life and the World

King Belshazzar uses the things dedicated to God for his own purposes and was celebrated for it.

- Why is it so easy to give misplaced honor and attention to those who flaunt their power?

- Where in our world do we see people misusing the things of God for their own good and not the glory of God?

- Do we see Christians tempted to manipulate the gifts of God for their own power and influence? If so, how?

Belshazzar praises the gods of gold, silver, bronze, iron, wood and stone instead of God when he toasts with the temple cups.

- How can we be mindful of undue praise we might be giving to the perishable things of this world?

- How does the interpretation of the written words give us guidance on how we should respond to idolatry and rebellion against God in our world today?

- What can we do to make sure we are living faithfully for the Lord our God? How does God help assure us or correct us in how faithfully we are living?

Daniel interprets the words written by the hand as a call for humility, especially for those in leadership.

- How are we to keep our pride in check?

- What does it look like for us to adopt a Christlike humility?

Close in prayer.

Challenges for Faithful Followers

SESSION 5

Session Outcome

To seek to grow in faith and consistency in our relationship with God.

Customize:

Daniel is the password to access expanded teaching helps on FoundryLeader.com

Discover:

Illustrated Bible Life discusses lions in the Bible, and gives verse-by-verse commentary on the Scripture passage.

September

29

REMAINING FAITHFUL TO GOD

Our faithful lives speak as loudly as our faithful words.

THE WORD

DANIEL 6:3-10

Now Daniel so distinguished himself among the administrators and the satraps by his exceptional qualities that the king planned to set him over the whole kingdom. ⁴At this, the administrators and the satraps tried to find grounds for charges against Daniel in his conduct of government affairs, but they were unable to do so. They could find no corruption in him, because he was trustworthy and neither corrupt nor negligent. ⁵Finally these men said, "We will never find any basis for charges against this man Daniel unless it has something to do with the law of his God."

⁶So these administrators and satraps went as a group to the king and said: "May King Darius live forever! ⁷The royal administrators, prefects, satraps, advisers and governors have all agreed that the king should issue an edict and enforce the decree that anyone who prays to any god or human being during the next thirty days, except to you, Your Majesty, shall be thrown into the lions' den. ⁸Now, Your Majesty, issue the decree and put it in writing so that it cannot be altered—in accordance with the law of the Medes and Persians, which cannot be repealed." ⁹So King Darius put the decree in writing.

KEY VERSE

¹⁰Now when Daniel learned that the decree had been published, he went home to his upstairs room where the windows opened toward Jerusalem. Three times a day he got down on his knees and prayed, giving thanks to his God, just as he had done before.

15-16

¹⁵Then the men went as a group to King Darius and said to him, "Remember, Your Majesty, that according to the law of the Medes and Persians no decree or edict that the king issues can be changed."

(handwritten annotation: GOVENORS)

Last Week:

We explored the ways arrogance is a sin against both God and others.

This Week:

We will explore the way our faithful lives must speak as loudly as our faithful words.

¹⁶So the king gave the order, and they brought Daniel and threw him into the lions' den. The king said to Daniel, "May your God, whom you serve continually, rescue you!"

19-23

¹⁹At the first light of dawn, the king got up and hurried to the lions' den. ²⁰When he came near the den, he called to Daniel in an anguished voice, "Daniel, servant of the living God, has your God, whom you serve continually, been able to rescue you from the lions?"

²¹Daniel answered, "May the king live forever! ²²My God sent his angel, and he shut the mouths of the lions. They have not hurt me, because I was found innocent in his sight. Nor have I ever done any wrong before you, Your Majesty."

²³The king was overjoyed and gave orders to lift Daniel out of the den. And when Daniel was lifted from the den, no wound was found on him, because he had trusted in his God.

ENGAGE THE WORD
FAITH OBSERVED

Daniel 6:3-5

Daniel's conduct spoke volumes to his contemporaries. He lived such an exemplary life that the king of Persia as well as his coworkers took notice. They observed his "exceptional qualities" (literally his "excellent spirit"), which included being "trustworthy and neither corrupt nor negligent" (vv. 3-4). That is to say, he did not deviate from his basic principles and could not be bought off. He remained diligently committed to his duties. These qualities made him the kind of person the king wanted administering his affairs. As a result, he planned to promote Daniel to a high position.

Not everyone was pleased with Daniel's good qualities however. These characteristics caused his fellow (jealous) administrators to look for a way to bring him down. The only thing they could find was "something to do with the law of his God" (v. 5), which they had noticed he followed closely. Surely these laws would come into conflict with the laws of the state. They were right, of course. The goals of the human institutions often differ from God's goals.

Unfortunately, those who follow the Lord are not

🔊 **Listen:**

FoundryLeader.com: This week's *Illustrated Bible Life* "Article Out Loud" surveys the role of lions in the ancient Near East.

Notes:

_____

_____

_____

_____

_____

_____

_____

_____

_____

_____

_____

_____

_____

_____

_____

_____

_____

_____

Did You Know?

The Persians developed one of the best organized empires the world has ever seen. The satrap system of administration reflected in this story allowed it to continue for over 200 years.

FAITH CHALLENGED

admired by everyone. Some people feel threatened when they see others live to please God. Jesus experienced this firsthand and warned His disciples, "If the world hates you, keep in mind that it hated me first" (John 15:18). When people notice that God's ways are not their ways, they often resent it.

Daniel 6:6-10

Daniel's enemies devised an ingenious plan to do away with him. They appealed to the king's sense of self-importance and proposed that all prayers to gods be directed through him for a month. Since Persian kings did not think of themselves as being divine, the point was that the king would become the sole mediator between heaven and earth. Those who did not submit to this decree would meet certain death in a den of hungry lions.

This set up a challenge between the law of Daniel's God and "the law of the Medes and Persians" (v. 8). The law by which Daniel lived stated that there should be "no other gods before" the Lord (Exodus 20:3). The law of the Persians called for acknowledging and submitting to all kinds of gods. The two laws came into direct conflict. If one were followed, the other would be broken.

Daniel chose to follow the law of his God and continued to do what he had been in the habit of doing: "He got down on his knees and prayed, giving thanks to his God" (v. 10). Though his decision to violate Persian law could not have been easy, his consistent discipline of daily prayer must have been less difficult. Daniel had "learned that the decree had been published" and understood what that meant (v. 10). He knew the consequences. But his spiritual discipline held him steady when the world challenged his beliefs.

Interestingly, we are told that Daniel was "giving thanks to his God" in his prayer time (v. 10). What could he possibly be thankful for? Was he thankful that God would be with him in this ordeal? Was

Discover:

The Asiatic lion was once common throughout the ancient Near East. Due to its unmatched power and majesty, the lion was a popular subject of artistic and literary expression. It's no surprise, then, that we find mention of a "den of lions" on the Persian palace grounds. What did the ancients think about this noble creature? Find out in this week's *Illustrated Bible Life* article, "The King of the Beasts."

Notes:

_____

_____

_____

_____

_____

_____

_____

_____

_____

_____

_____

_____

_____

_____

_____

_____

_____

_____

_____

Session 5

Think About It

The only time Daniel speaks in this story is in the lion's den. His actions communicated more about his faith than his words. Both the king and his accusers clearly saw his beliefs in how he lived.

FAITH REWARDED

he thankful for an opportunity to witness for God through this circumstance? Whatever Daniel may have been thinking, he does not say. We only know what he did. He continued to talk with God and give thanks.

Daniel 6:15-16, 19-23

Daniel's enemies noticed his defiance of the Persian edict and immediately reported it to the king. However, the king did not move quickly. Instead of being angry, he looked for a way to save Daniel because he knew his value. But, in the end, he could not rescue him. The law designed to exalt the king actually ended up oppressing him. Even the king could not overturn his own law.

Humanly speaking, Daniel had no chance of surviving a den of lions. Yet, the king expressed some hope when he called out to Daniel, "May your God, whom you serve continually, rescue you" (v. 16). Was this wishful thinking or an earnest prayer? Whatever his intent, the king received his answer early the next morning. He called into the pit and heard Daniel respond, "My God sent his angel and shut the mouths of the lions" (v. 22). When the Persians closed the mouth of the den, the Lord closed the mouths of the lions.

Daniel emerged from the pit of certain death without a scratch. "He had trusted in his God" and God came through (v. 23). The story never indicates that he expected to be delivered. He simply remained faithful and trusted that God ruled regardless of circumstances. As a result, the king observed that Daniel's God was "the living God," not a dead or distracted god (v. 20). Daniel's God actually responded to people and made a difference in their lives. The truth of God's goodness became evident to the world through the faithful actions of his servant.

REFLECT Are you currently in a "lion's den"? If so, in what ways can your life be an expression of your faithfulness toward God?

JIM EDLIN

Discussion Guide

 Connect to My Experience

Begin your session by asking,

- What does it mean to be consistent in something?

- What are the things in your life where it is the most important for you to be consistent?

- What are the benefits of being consistent?

Consistency does not necessarily mean we stay the same. Being consistent daily can, and should, lead to growth.

- How can consistency grow us?

- Where in your life has consistency made a positive difference? How did it feel to see how you had grown?

Transition:

Whatever his circumstance, we find Daniel always trusting, seeking the Lord's wisdom. Today's story shows God's faithfulness and the ways Daniel's constant walk with God has strengthened his faith, even in the face of death.

Connect to the Word

Invite someone to read Daniel 6:3-5, then discuss the following,

Daniel had "distinguished himself among the administrators and the satraps by his exceptional qualities." In light of this, there arose a plot against Daniel by the administrators and satraps.

- Although we are not exactly told the reason at this point (see v. 13), but why do you think they conspired against Daniel?

- In what ways can jealousy and envy lead us to ungodly actions toward others?

- What does it say about Daniel that his opponents have difficulty finding grounds for charges against him?

The administrators and the satraps have to find a way to use Daniel's faith as grounds for charges against him.

- How do you think the administrators and satraps know about Daniel's faith in God? In what ways is Daniel's faith public enough that they even considered it as a way to trap him?

Invite someone to read Daniel 6:6-10, then discuss the following,

Daniel's opponents go to King Darius and ask him to throw anyone praying to anyone or anything except the king during the next 30 days into the lion's den. Darius agrees.

- In what way can power blind a leader from seeing the consequences of his/her actions?

- What law of God might make it possible for Daniel's opponents to set him up for punishment from the king? (God's commands begin with exclusive worship of Him: "You shall have no other gods before me" [Exodus 20:3].)

"Three times a day he got down on his knees and prayed, giving thanks to his God, just as he had done before" (v.10).

- What conclusions can we make about Daniel's faith in God based on his actions?

Insight

Daniel prayed three times a day by his window facing Jerusalem. As Daniel is in exile, this not only pictures his dedicated faith, but also his longing to go home and see Jerusalem restored.

Invite someone to read Daniel 6:15-16, 19-23, then discuss the following,

■ Why do you think that Daniel gives thanks to God despite the circumstance he is facing?

The officials go to the king and, manipulating the situation, inform him that Daniel has broken the law. On hearing this news, the king, "was greatly distressed" and "was determined to rescue Daniel and made every effort until sundown to save him" (v. 14).

■ Why do you think the king's initial response to this news, rather than anger, was distress?

■ What kind of impact might Daniel have had on the king's life?

Daniel was thrown into the lion's den and the entrance was sealed.

■ What do you think Daniel could have done to save himself from the king's punishment?

■ From the onlooker's perspective, what chance does Daniel possibly have in the lion's den?

■ From this story, what can we learn about the differences between a worldly perspective and a faith perspective?

God rescues Daniel by shutting the lion's mouths. Daniel simply trusts!

■ How might this remind us of the other stories of Daniel we have read? How was God consistently faithful in Daniel's life? In what ways had God's power and wisdom been sufficient for Daniel's situation?

The men who had falsely accused Daniel were tossed into the lions' den, along with their families (v. 24).

■ In what ways can our actions have far-reaching effects beyond ourselves?

Connect to My Life and the World

Daniel's life of faith was so visible that his opponents tried to use it against him.

■ What are some of the ways that we practice our faith that have a noticeable effect on our everyday life?

■ How do our faithful actions testify to others about the kind of God we serve?

■ What kind of message does it send to others if we are inconsistent in our faith when trouble arises?

Daniel teaches us by example that no matter what we face, we can place our faith in God, knowing He is with us.

■ How do we keep our faith consistent like Daniel? In what ways can we love God consistently as Christians?

■ What does Daniel's story teach us about how God rewards and helps the faithful? How does God help us to keep the faith and stay the course of our spiritual journey?

■ God can and does deliver us from "the lion's den" times of life. However, what happens when God does not?

Close in prayer.

Unit 1

Challenges for Faithful Followers

Session Outcome

To trust that God remains in control of this world even as kingdoms—good and bad—rise and fall.

Customize:

Daniel is the password to access expanded teaching helps on FoundryLeader.com

 **Discover:**

Illustrated Bible Life explores the language of "son of man" in Daniel and its connection to Jesus, and gives verse-by-verse commentary on the Scripture passage.

October

6

DEALING WITH EVIL KINGDOMS

Though earthly kingdoms rise and fall, God continues to reign over His world.

THE WORD

DANIEL 7:2-9

Daniel said: "In my vision at night I looked, and there before me were the four winds of heaven churning up the great sea. ³Four great beasts, each different from the others, came up out of the sea.

⁴"The first was like a lion, and it had the wings of an eagle. I watched until its wings were torn off and it was lifted from the ground so that it stood on two feet like a human being, and the mind of a human was given to it.

⁵"And there before me was a second beast, which looked like a bear. It was raised up on one of its sides, and it had three ribs in its mouth between its teeth. It was told, 'Get up and eat your fill of flesh!'

⁶"After that, I looked, and there before me was another beast, one that looked like a leopard. And on its back it had four wings like those of a bird. This beast had four heads, and it was given authority to rule.

⁷"After that, in my vision at night I looked, and there before me was a fourth beast—terrifying and frightening and very powerful. It had large iron teeth; it crushed and devoured its victims and trampled underfoot whatever was left. It was different from all the former beasts, and it had ten horns.

⁸"While I was thinking about the horns, there before me was another horn, a little one, which came up among them; and three of the first horns were uprooted before it. This horn had eyes like the eyes of a human being and a mouth that spoke boastfully.

⁹"As I looked, "thrones were set in place, and the Ancient of Days took his seat. His clothing was as white as snow; the hair of his head was white like wool. His throne was flaming with fire, and its wheels were all ablaze.

Last Week:

We recognized that people know how authentic our faith is by how we live, not just by how we say we live.

This Week:

We will recognize that God's faithful people find comfort in knowing God's kingdom is always present and will continue forever despite the prevalent evil in the world.

11-14

¹¹"Then I continued to watch because of the boastful words the horn was speaking. I kept looking until the beast was slain and its body destroyed and thrown into the blazing fire. ¹²(The other beasts had been stripped of their authority, but were allowed to live for a period of time.)

¹³"In my vision at night I looked, and there before me was one like a son of man, coming with the clouds of heaven. He approached the Ancient of Days and was led into his presence. **¹⁴He was given authority, glory and sovereign power; all nations and peoples of every language worshiped him. His dominion is an everlasting dominion that will not pass away, and his kingdom is one that will never be destroyed.**

KEY VERSE

ENGAGE THE WORD

THE CHAOS OF EVIL KINGDOMS

Daniel 7:2-8

God gave Daniel a glimpse of what earthly kingdoms look like from heaven's perspective. With dramatic images, Daniel's vision portrays the kingdoms of this world as brutally destructive and terrifying. Each one emerges from the windswept, chaotic waters of the ocean displaying its own special brand of power and terror. The three most feared wild beasts represent the first three kingdoms: a lion, a bear, and a leopard. Each is malformed in some way to intensify its terror. The fourth beast cannot compare to anything in this world because it is even more horrifying than the first three. This kingdom ruthlessly "crushed and devoured its victims and trampled underfoot whatever was left" (v. 7). Its many "horns" seem to signify its different rulers, who rise and fall just like the kingdom over which they rule (v. 8).

Whether these beasts were meant to symbolize particular nations or all earthly kingdoms in general, they relate important messages as a group. First, we see that human governments tend to oppress rather than empower people. They exploit, devour, and crush their subjects. Further, as one realm replaces another, they become increasingly frightening and oppressive.

Notes:

_____

_____

_____

_____

_____

_____

_____

_____

_____

_____

_____

_____

_____

_____

_____

_____

_____

Watch:

Dr. Jim Edlin introduces this session on dealing with evil kingdoms.

Listen:

FoundryLeader.com: This week's *Illustrated Bible Life* "Article Out Loud" takes a close look at messianic prophecy in Daniel.

Notes:

_____

_____

_____

_____

_____

_____

_____

_____

_____

_____

_____

_____

_____

_____

_____

Did You Know?

The visions in the latter part of Daniel reaffirm the stories in the first part. Together they assure God's people that God remains fully in control of this world both now and into the future.

THE JUSTICE OF GOD'S KINGDOM

Rather than improve they decline. Such a picture of human governance should not surprise us however. Power in the hands of sinful people always leads to disaster. We have witnessed it over and over again throughout world history. Without God human institutions always generate confusion, eventually destroy the beautiful world God intended, and ultimately fail.

Daniel 7:9, 11-12

With verse 9 the scene changes abruptly from chaos to calm. The justness of God's benevolent rule contrasts sharply with the horror of human governance. God comes to judge the kingdoms of this world sitting upon a throne as the unquestioned Ruler over all. He is called "the Ancient of Days" to underscore the long-standing authority by which He rules humankind (v. 9). God has been there from the beginning and even before any earthly kingdom. His white clothing and hair, along with "his throne ... flaming with fire and its wheels ... all ablaze," add to the impression of God's sovereign control and right to judge humanity (v. 9).

Each beast of earth submits to God's judgment. The most threatening beast, the fourth one, is "slain and its body destroyed" (v. 11). All its evil power is erased. The other three beasts are "stripped of their authority" so that they no longer threaten people (v. 12). Those who devoured others are consumed by God's inescapable judgment.

At this point, Daniel caught a vision of what God has done and promises to do throughout the Bible. As Isaiah explained, when God is ready to do so, "the LORD will march out like a champion, like a warrior he will stir up his zeal; with a shout he will raise the battle cry and will triumph over his enemies" (Isaiah 42:13). God's passion for this world means He will not allow evil to triumph in it. He will bring down those who destroy His creation and cause chaos. Evil does not have the final word in God's world.

 **Discover:**

Among the better-known messianic prophecies in the Old Testament is Daniel 7:13, particularly the words, "I looked, and there before me was *one like a son of man,* coming with the clouds of heaven" (emphasis added). For us Christians, the connection to Jesus seems obvious; to the Jews of Daniel's day however, not so much. How are we to interpret this language in Daniel? Let's find out in this week's *Illustrated Bible Life* article, "One Like a Son of Man."

Session 6

Think About It

Both chapter 2 and chapter 7 give dramatic images of earthly kingdoms. The impressive statue of chapter 2 views them from a human perspective, while the terrifying beasts of chapter 7 sees them from God's.

THE BEAUTY OF GOD'S KINGDOM

Daniel 7:13-14

Following the judgment of the beasts, a beautiful scene emerges. God inaugurates a new ruler to govern a new kingdom in this world. In contrast to the kingdoms of the beasts, His kingdom "is an everlasting dominion that will not pass away" (v 14). While human realms always come to an end, this kingdom never does. Order and permanence mark this new kingdom.

The new ruler of God's kingdom is described as "one like a son of man, coming on the clouds of heaven" (v. 13). This is exactly how Jesus described himself in Matthew 24:30. In addition, Jesus regularly referred to himself as "the Son of Man" throughout His life on earth. In this way He identified himself with the one Daniel envisioned in this passage. Though He was human (a son of man), He was also divine (coming on the clouds of heaven). As a result, "all nations and peoples of every language worshiped him" (v. 14).

Jesus proclaimed the fulfillment of Daniel's vision when He preached that "the kingdom of heaven has come near" (Matthew 4:17). The kingdom envisioned by Daniel became reality in Jesus and only awaited His second coming to appear in all its fullness. The kingdom that "will never be destroyed" arrived among us when Jesus came to earth (v. 14).

This vision encouraged people in Daniel's world not to be overly concerned about evil human kingdoms, whether Babylonian, Persian, or some other entity. Those kingdoms would eventually fall. God would judge them and someday remove them from this world. The same is true for us today, yet even more so. God's kingdom has already come into our world. Jesus reigns now and His kingdom will never end.

REFLECT Today, thank God for being the Ruler over heaven and earth.

JIM EDLIN

Discussion Guide

Connect to My Experience

Begin your session by asking,

- Do you have pets? Would you consider your pets to be well trained? What did it take for them to listen to your voice?

- Have you ever encountered a dangerous animal? If so, how did you feel in that moment? Was that animal inside or outside of its cage? What made this encounter scary or dangerous?

Transition:

Daniel, who often interpreted the dreams of others, had his own visions which speak to the power of God over the most terrifying of powers and principalities.

Connect to the Word

Invite someone to read Daniel 7:2-8, then discuss the following,

Daniel's vision takes place at night and opens with a view of the sea, with winds blowing from every direction. Out of this, four beasts rise.

- How is "the sea" often depicted in Scripture? (Often symbolizes uncertainty and disorder. See Revelation 21:1.)

- What other scriptures might remind us of this picture? (One example is the beginning of the creation narrative in Genesis 1. The Spirit hovers on the waters. The world before God speaks is chaotic, formless, and void.)

The beasts emerge from the chaos and in the darkness.

- What do you notice about the beasts' features? What kind of commands and authority are they given?

- The fourth beast is particularly fearsome. What makes it scarier than the other beasts? What does Daniel notice most about it? What does the smallest horn do and why do you think this is significant?

Invite someone to read Daniel 7:9, 11-12, then discuss the following,

Prophecy is not primarily for telling the future but communicating the commands, nature, and character of God, which often contrasts with the powers of the world.

- What does Daniel's vision tell us about God? How does he describe God? How does he describe the throne of God?

The term "Ancient of Days" (only found in this chapter: vv. 9, 13, 22) signifies God is eternal and has authority to rule. The white clothing and fire signify God's holiness.

- Why do you think it is significant that God is described in this way?

In verse 11, Daniel's attention is drawn back to the fourth beast because it is loudly speaking boastful words.

- What happens to this beast and his horns? What happens to the other beasts?

- Who defeats the beasts and strips them of authority? (It is implied that the Ancient of Days strikes them down.)

These mighty and fearsome beasts are suddenly gone in two verses of Scripture!

- What is the significance of how little time it takes to describe their destruction? What can this tell us about God's power over them?

Insight

As far back as the creation story, the chaos cannot fight back against God. God says, "let there be light" and chaos gives way to creation. The beasts who rise from chaos are destroyed without a battle because they have no power over the Ancient of Days.

Invite someone to read Daniel 7:13-14, then discuss the following,

Daniel's attention now fully turns to see one who is like a son of man being brought into the presence of the Ancient of Days.

- In what ways does this "son of man" compare to the beasts? (The "son of man" seems much less intimidating, but has all the authority, power, and honor.)

- How does the kingdom of the "son of man" compare to the reign of the beasts? (Consider how the son of man's kingdom includes all the nations and how it is everlasting, where the beasts were defeated so quickly.)

- Which of these kingdoms seem to be better for the people living in them?

- How do we see Jesus, who is called the "Son of Man" and "Son of God," reflected in this passage? (See Isaiah 9:1-6; 11:1-5; Micah 5:1-5; Zechariah 9:9-10; and Philippians 2:6-7, 10-11. See also, Matthew 20:28; Mark 14:62; Luke 19:10; and John 3:13.)

[Encourage your group to read Daniel 7:15-28 this week.]

Invite someone to read Revelation 7:9-12, then discuss the following,

This vision of the kingdom of God fully established with Jesus Christ (the Lamb of God) on the throne should remind us of Daniel's vision!

- How is the image in Revelation similar to how Daniel describes the vision of the one who is "like a son of man, coming on the clouds of heaven"?

Connect to My Life and the World

While we do not know if in today's passage there was an intended connection to specific earthly kingdoms; we can draw some general similarities to the world today.

- How does the way that earthly kingdoms and nations use their power compare with the beasts in Daniel's vision?

- How do the powers of our world today devour and boast? What contemporary misuse of power troubles you the most?

- How do Christians usually react to the sinfulness of our world today? When we hear news of "beastly" behavior in the world, how should we react?

Think about the name Daniel gives for God in this vision: "The Ancient of Days."

- What significance can this name for God have for us today? (God has been reigning long before the problems that we face today and will reign for eternity. He is Ancient of Days! He is eternal; the beasts are temporary.)

- What kind of encouragement does today's passage give you for what you are troubled by today? How does this change the way that we live from day to day?

- How do we keep our eyes focused on our living and reigning God and away from the boastful "horn" of the beasts in the world?

- Jesus already sits at the right hand of God the Father. Jesus has already won the victory over sin and death! How can we share the encouraging news that our God reigns?

Close in prayer.

Session Outcome

To develop a prayer life that includes praying for our faith communities to pursue God's goal of holy living.

Customize:

Daniel is the password to access expanded teaching helps on FoundryLeader.com

 **Discover:**

Illustrated Bible Life takes a look at how the book of Daniel uses numbers, and provides verse-by-verse commentary on the Scripture passage.

Unit 1

Challenges for Faithful Followers

October

13

A REPENTANT PROPHET AND A RESPONSIVE GOD

We can intercede on behalf of our Christian communities for the good of God's kingdom.

THE WORD

DANIEL 9:1-9

In the first year of Darius son of Xerxes (a Mede by descent), who was made ruler over the Babylonian kingdom—²in the first year of his reign, I, Daniel, understood from the Scriptures, according to the word of the LORD given to Jeremiah the prophet, that the desolation of Jerusalem would last seventy years. ³So I turned to the LORD God and pleaded with him in prayer and petition, in fasting, and in sackcloth and ashes.

⁴I prayed to the LORD my God and confessed:

"LORD, the great and awesome God, who keeps his covenant of love with those who love him and keep his commandments, ⁵we have sinned and done wrong. We have been wicked and have rebelled; we have turned away from your commands and laws. ⁶We have not listened to your servants the prophets, who spoke in your name to our kings, our princes and our ancestors, and to all the people of the land.

⁷"LORD, you are righteous, but this day we are covered with shame—the people of Judah and the inhabitants of Jerusalem and all Israel, both near and far, in all the countries where you have scattered us because of our unfaithfulness to you. ⁸We and our kings, our princes and our ancestors are covered with shame, LORD, because we have sinned against you. ⁹The LORD our God is merciful and forgiving, even though we have rebelled against him;

17-19

¹⁷"Now, our God, hear the prayers and petitions of your servant. For your sake, LORD, look with favor on your desolate sanctuary. ¹⁸Give ear, our God, and hear; open your eyes and see the desolation of the city that bears your Name. We do not make requests of you because

Last Week:

We examined how kingdoms of this world come and go, but God's sovereignty remains steadfast.

This Week:

We will examine how God's people are called to pray for the purity of God's people.

Session 7

we are righteous, but because of your great mercy. ¹⁹Lᴏʀᴅ, listen! Lᴏʀᴅ, forgive! Lᴏʀᴅ, hear and act! For your sake, my God, do not delay, because your city and your people bear your Name."

21-24

²¹while I was still in prayer, Gabriel, the man I had seen in the earlier vision, came to me in swift flight about the time of the evening sacrifice. ²²He instructed me and said to me, "Daniel, I have now come to give you insight and understanding. **²³As soon as you began to pray, a word went out, which I have come to tell you, for you are highly esteemed. Therefore, consider the word and understand the vision:**

KEY VERSES

²⁴"Seventy 'sevens' are decreed for your people and your holy city to finish transgression, to put an end to sin, to atone for wickedness, to bring in everlasting righteousness, to seal up vision and prophecy and to anoint the Most Holy Place.

ENGAGE THE WORD

DANIEL'S CALL TO INTERCESSION

Daniel 9:1-3

Anytime is a good time to pray. But certain occasions call for more intense prayer than others. This was one of those times for Daniel. His reading of Jeremiah's prophecy had led to new understanding. Through Jeremiah, God had said that Judah would "serve the king of Babylon seventy years" and "when seventy years are completed for Babylon, I will come to you and ... bring you back to this place" (Jeremiah 25:11 and 29:10). Daniel noted that "the first year" of Persian rule in 539 BC had ended almost seventy years of Babylonian domination of Judah (v. 1). Perhaps it was time for God to fulfill His promise to Daniel's people.

The Babylonian conquest of Judah had been devastating for its people as well as for God's reputation. Jerusalem and its temple had been leveled to the ground. A large portion of Judah's population had been killed or displaced over the Middle East. Many, including Daniel, had been forced to live in exile in Babylon for generations. Because of this, people of the world viewed Israel's God as weak and irrelevant.

🔊 **Listen:**

FoundryLeader.com: This week's *Illustrated Bible Life* "Article Out Loud" explores the symbolism behind the numbers in the book of Daniel.

Notes:

_____

_____

_____

_____

_____

_____

_____

_____

_____

_____

_____

_____

_____

_____

_____

Did You Know?
Numbers in Daniel were symbolic and not meant to be calculated. Seventy is the perfect number times 10. It symbolizes a complete amount of time, like a full life in which a person might see several generations of descendants.

DANIEL'S PRAYER OF INTERCESSION

They dismissed testimonies of His compassion and grace as well as His claim to supremacy.

Realizing this crucial moment in Israel's history, when the fortunes of God and His people could change, Daniel sought the Lord earnestly. He fasted and put on mourning clothes of "sackcloth and ashes" to indicate his desperate desire for God's intervention (v. 3).

Daniel 9:4-9, 17-19

Daniel's prayer highlights the stark contrast between the awesomeness of God and the awfulness of sin. Throughout the prayer, the prophet addresses God as "Lord" *(adonai),* a name that affirms God's sovereign command over this world (v 4). He remains in full control of every part of creation regardless of what circumstances might suggest. God is especially "great and awesome" because He "keeps his covenant of love" with His people (v. 3). God graciously engaged Abraham and his descendants in a binding love relationship. This is why Daniel also addresses God as "our God" (vv. 9, 10, 13, 14, 15, 17, 18). He and his people belonged to God, and God belonged to them.

Throughout the centuries God had remained faithful to His commitment to the covenant even though Israel had not. Daniel confessed their unfaithfulness in every way he could think to say it. They have "sinned ... done wrong ... been wicked ... rebelled ... turned away" and "not listened" (vv. 5-6). That just about covers it all. As the first term "sinned" suggests, they missed God's best for their lives. As a result, they were "covered with shame" (v. 7). They had embarrassed themselves as well as God.

Daniel admitted that God was right to send His people into exile. That was only fair. But Daniel also knew that God was "merciful and forgiving" (v. 9). So, on this basis, he pleaded for God to "listen . . . forgive . . . hear and act" (v. 19). Though God was right to put His people in exile, God would also be right to show

Discover:

In a book like Daniel, numbers do more than just count and measure things. They also point to truths beyond their literal use in the story. The challenge is to know when this is happening and to interpret what it means. How do we do this? This week's *Illustrated Bible Life* article, "Daniel by the Numbers," explains.

Notes:

Think About It

Israel's prophets found spiritual insight from reading the words of other prophets. In their messages, they frequently alluded to earlier prophets like Moses, Hosea, Isaiah, and Jeremiah.

GOD'S RESPONSE TO INTERCESSION

mercy. That is also in keeping with who God is. He is the God of "great mercy" (v. 18).

Daniel 9:21-24

Daniel received an immediate response from God. It was even delivered by an angel. However, the answer was not exactly what he wanted to hear nor as clear as he might have hoped it would be. Judgment for sin was not over and the day of full redemption remained somewhere in the future.

The details about the future were puzzling, but the main point of God's message was crystal clear. The angel explained that "seventy 'sevens' are decreed for your people" before God would restore His kingdom on earth (v. 24). That is to say, it would be a long time before things were set right again. The time when Daniel's people would "finish transgression" remained some time away (v. 24). As a result, the day of "everlasting righteousness" would be put off (v. 24). How long this would be is not clearly spelled out. "Seventy 'sevens'" simply conveyed an indefinite amount of time.

So, Daniel did not get all his questions answered, just like many of us have experienced. God did not give the prophet a blueprint of how the future might unfold. Yet, God did clarify what He desired from His people. God wanted them "to finish transgression" and "put an end to sin" (v 24). He was looking for a holy people, as He always has. .

The day of final and full salvation remains somewhere in the future. In the meantime, we can pray like Daniel for our friends and neighbors. We can ask God to make us holy people in preparation for the day when He finally rules supreme over this world and the day of "everlasting righteousness" finally dawns (v. 24).

REFLECT Who can you breathe an intercessory prayer for today?

JIM EDLIN

Discussion Guide

Connect to My Experience

As Christians, it is safe to assume that we affirm prayer as an important part of our life. This is true, but it is also necessary to be reminded *why* we pray.

- How would you describe the reason for prayer? Why is it important?

- What does your prayer life look like? What do you find yourself praying about the most lately?

- How does prayer deepen your relationship with God? How does it affect you personally in everyday living?

Transition:

Today, we get a snapshot of Daniel's prayer life. His cry to God shows his heart for the people of God's restoration and helps lead us in how we can seek the Lord in prayer.

Connect to the Word

Invite someone to read Daniel 9:1-3, then discuss the following,

Daniel gains insight from the words of Jeremiah the prophet about the defeat of Jerusalem and the exile of the Israelites in Babylon. His response is to pray to God.

- What does Daniel's posture of prayer tell us about his reaction to this insight? What role does our posture have in our prayers?

Invite someone to read Daniel 9:4-9, 17-19, then discuss the following,

Daniel does not begin his prayer with what is needed, but with confession. Confession does not simply talk about things that we have done wrong. It is about affirming the things that we believe are true. Daniel starts and ends his prayer by confessing what is true about God.

- What are the things that Daniel believes about God?

- What words does Daniel use to describe God?

- Why does Daniel emphasize God's character in his prayer? How can focusing on God's glory, righteousness, and love help center our prayer?

Daniel goes on to confess the truth of the wrongs done by God's people.

- What is it that the people of God have done wrong? What commandments have they broken?

Daniel says that God is merciful and forgiving (v. 9) despite their disobedience (vv. 10-11); but, he also lists the consequences of their disobedience (v. 14).

- What does this tell us about God? What does this tell us about sin?

- In every confession of sin, Daniel says, "we," including himself with the rest of the people of Israel and their wicked deeds. Why do you think he says "we" instead of "they" when talking about the sins of Israel?

Then, after confession, Daniel turns to his requests.

- What does Daniel ask God for?

- What about God's nature and character gives Daniel the confidence to make these requests of God?

- What do you think Daniel meant by praying, "We do not make requests of you because we are righteous, but because of your great mercy" (v. 18)?

Invite someone to read Daniel 9:21-24, then discuss the following,

Daniel receives an answer, from an angel of the Lord, to his prayer.

Insight

"The prophet, Jeremiah, mentions the 'seventy-years' of desolation for Jerusalem in Jeremiah 25:1-11 where he prophesied that Nebuchadnezzar would destroy Jerusalem. He also mentions it in Jeremiah 29:1-11 and urges the people to accept this and be faithful for the long-run in their exile."[1]

■ Why might it be significant that the angel says to Daniel, "As soon as you began to pray, a word went out"? (Consider that it is not because of the content of Daniel's words but his faithful act of praying that prompted a word from the Lord. God hears Daniel and sends a reply because God loves Daniel and His people.)

God is working toward the good of the people's future—even though they rebelled—to finish transgression, end sin, atone for wickedness, and bring everlasting righteousness.

■ Can this hope of God apply to every prayer? If so, how?

Daniel is not given a time limit for exile. Scholars are not in exact agreement on the meaning of "seventy-sevens," whenever that is (a long period of time), God will set things right even as God sets the people's hearts on the right track.

■ What does it mean for the time being that the people will remain in exile?

■ Even though going home was not in the near future, how do you think the people could start living into God's call to turn from sin and live in righteousness, even while they are still in Babylon?

 ## Connect to My Life and the World

While prayer can happen on any occasion, Daniel's decision to pray in this passage begins with studying Scripture.

■ What role does the Bible have in your prayer life? What would it look like to read Scripture expecting that it will guide us to the Lord in prayer?

When Daniel prays to God, he confesses both his faith and his people's sin.

■ What role does confession have in our faith life? Does our confession in our prayers express what we believe about God? (Consider how the Lord's Prayer opens with a confession of faith: "Our Father, in heaven, holy is your name.")

■ Do you think that it is important to affirm who God is in your prayers? Why or why not?

It is also important to confess to God when we have done something wrong against Him or our neighbor.

■ How do we know when we have done wrong? From where do we get this feeling of conviction when we sin?

■ What does it look like to pray for forgiveness as a community?

■ If God is already aware when we sin, why is it important to pray about it?

Daniel has to wait for God to set things right. God is leading the people toward an end to their sin and a start to everlasting righteousness. Yet, they wait in Babylon for that day.

■ How are we waiting for a similar answer as Christians? (God desires this for the whole world and Jesus has won the victory, but we wait for the kingdom to be fully established on earth.)

Close in prayer.

1. Barry L. Ross, *Daniel*, in the *Reading and Interpreting the Bible Series*, (Kansas City: The Foundry Publishing, 2023), 168.

A Closer Look at the Book of Esther

Introduction to Esther

The book of Esther is one of those surprising Old Testament accounts. It tells of a plot to destroy the Jewish people living under Persian rule during the time of Xerxes (ZUHRK-seez; 486-465 BC; also known as Ahasuerus, uh-haz-yoo-EHR-russ). It contains the heroic actions of how two brave people averted a holocaust.

The result was the institution of Purim, a Jewish celebration remembering the defeat of their enemies and the continued existence of the Jewish people. This festival, held on the 14th and 15th days of the Jewish month of Adar (usually March), is the most joyous and festive of the Jewish holidays. The focus of this article centers on the surprises and sacred messages found in this often-overlooked sacred writing.

Surprises

When one compares the book of Esther to the rest of the Old Testament, two surprising facts come to the foreground. The first is this: the book focuses on, and is named for, a woman. For 21st-century western readers, that may not raise an eyebrow. However, to the patriarchal audience who first read this book, this was quite astounding! Only one other biblical book has this distinction: Ruth. In that book, non-Jewish Ruth marries Jewish Boaz. They had a son, Obed, the grandfather of King David. Nearly a thousand years later, Mary gave birth to Jesus, who was of the house and lineage of David (Luke 2:4)—and Ruth!

The book of Esther tells the story of a remarkable woman, Esther, who lived approximately 450 years before the birth of Jesus. On the advice of her cousin Mordecai, Esther concealed her Jewish identity when she was taken to become part of the Persian king's harem. She was so beautiful and pleasing to the king that he made her his queen.

Her high position in the court enabled Esther to intercede for her people—though at the risk of her own life—when Mordecai discovered a plot to destroy the Jewish people. Because of her heroic action, the king destroyed the plotters, and allowed the Jews to defend themselves against their attackers.

The second surprise is that the author never mentions God. Both Jews and Christians have debated how a book that never mentions God, but rather concentrates on the schemes of people, could be worthy of sacred status. Yet, though the unknown author never mentioned God, the book depicts a series of "strange coincidences" that might help us to understand why both Jews and Christians ultimately affirmed the canonical status of this book.

- The king happened to choose Esther above all the other women (2:17).
- Mordecai happened to hear about the plot to kill the king and warned him (2:21-23).
- The scribes happened to write Mordecai's warning in the Royal Chronicle (2:23).
- The king happened to decide to see Esther instead of allowing her execution (5:3).
- The king could not sleep one night and asked for a reading of the royal chronicles, where he happened to discover Mordecai's warning (6:1-2).
- Because Esther happened to be queen, she was able to tell the king about Haman's plot to destroy the Jews in time to avert the plot (chap. 7). The king allowed the Jews to defend themselves, which resulted in their defeating those who had set out to destroy them (chaps. 8—9).

Haman's plot to destroy the Jewish people highlights another coincidence. Haman was a descendant of Agag (3:1), the Amalekite king who fought against Saul (1 Sam. 15). From the exodus through the reign of Hezekiah, these two nations had warred against each other. The Persian plot was one episode in that long history.

Without once mentioning God, the author of the book of Esther nonetheless depicts the hand of the Divine Deliverer working behind the scenes.

Sacred Messages

The book of Esther highlights two important truths for God's people. The first is that God is at work, often behind the scenes, for the good of His people. The book of Esther should bring comfort to those who feel they are fighting their battles all alone: God is always working on behalf of those who love him (Rom. 8:28).

The climactic exchange between Mordecai and Esther in 4:14-16 contains the second message. Mordecai raised the memorable question to Esther, "Who knows but that you have come to royal position for such a time as this?" Esther replied, "I will go to the king. . . . And if I perish, I perish." The point is this: God is the One who brings salvation; yet, often that salvation is brought to the human scene through the obedient and courageous actions of a few faithful people. Moses, Mordecai, Esther, the three Hebrew children, the apostles, Paul—Scripture relates the accounts of those who stood up and said, "I will follow God, and if I perish, I perish." The challenge for 21st-century believers, surrounded by such a great cloud of witnesses, is to run the same race, looking to Jesus, the Author and Finisher of our faith (Heb. 12:1-2).

RONALD V. COMPTON is an ordained elder in the Church of the Nazarene

Female Dynamics in Esther

The book of Esther contains two named women who are essential to the unfolding story. Because of their presence, the book is full of power and gender-role reversals. Patriarchal cultures are strategically structured to benefit men, especially in the ways in which men wield positions of power and authority. As a result, women in the ancient Near East had very little power and were regarded as the property of men. However, sometimes women directly challenged the patriarchal structure. This is especially seen through Queen Vashti (Esther 1). On the other hand, Esther more often strategically and subversively worked around the power system via means of wit and manipulation.

The narrative begins with Queen Vashti's deliberate and defiant refusal to obey her husband, King Xerxes. His request for her to appear before the noblemen was a means of objectification and control. After all, he had just finished showing off all his other possessions, and in accordance with his patriarchal culture, Vashti was also his property to flaunt (Esther 1:1-6). According to Persian custom, women could be present at banquets before the drinking began (see Nehemiah 2:6). At Belshazzar's banquet, only women from the king's harem were present (Daniel 5:2). Thus, summoning Vashti not only diminished her role as the king's "property," but further denigrated her status by presenting her as a mere concubine. Vashti's refusal challenged Xerxes in two ways. First, it usurped the power Xerxes wielded as king. But secondly, it also challenged her culture's familial power a husband had over his wife. For this reason, Vashti's defiance was viewed as a threat to all men in the entire kingdom. In the eyes of the insecure rulers, her "no" signaled a social rebellion they were eager to quickly quell (1:13-20). As a result, Vashti was sent away and disappeared into the background. It is unclear whether she was executed or exiled (1:19). Challenging the king's power had painful consequences for Vashti, yet her bravery put a story in motion to save God's people.

Unfortunately, Vashti was not the only woman who suffered at the hands of an oppressive patriarchal culture: the story mentions many unnamed women who endured similar fates. As a means of regaining his power over his kingdom and, practically, to choose a new wife, King Xerxes brought all the virgins in the kingdom to the palace. Women were considered marriageable when they began their menstrual cycles, so it is likely that they were young teenagers. As indicated by 1:13-14, each woman spent one night with the king and then was sent back to the harem, where she would remain for the rest of her life. These young, nameless women had no social, political, or gender power over this situation and were unable to resist the king's wanton desires, on which each of their fates hinged.

Esther was one of these young women taken into the king's ha-rem, and while we do not know what she thought or felt about her circumstances, she had no power to defy the king. What she wanted was of no interest and she was not consulted before being brought to the king's bed (2:14). The king's elevation of Esther to her position as queen did not undo the sexual abuse wrought against her. And while God did not compel the king to abuse his station, God nevertheless redeemed this traumatic experience for Esther.

At first, Esther appears to be the "perfect wife," at least according to ancient Near Eastern patriarchal standards. Like Vashti, she was beautiful, but unlike the former queen, Esther was obedient and passive, obeying both her uncle, Mordecai, and the king. She did not ask the eunuch for anything additional (2:15) and was hesitant to approach the king against his wishes (4:11). In fact, throughout the narrative Esther is presented as passively "taken" by others (2:8, 16). Yet, upon further investigation, Esther demonstrates subversive resilience. She uses the limited power she has as a woman and queen to challenge the plot to murder God's people.

The turning point in Esther's character development occurs in Esther 4:15-16. Here, for the first time, Esther issued a command. Using direct, imperative language, Esther took control and emerged as both a political and religious leader over her people. Esther devised a plan of her own, one that was much more cunning than the one Mordecai proposed (see 4:8). Whereas Vashti refused to come to the king, Esther intruded on the king. And although the king ordered Esther to explain her reasons for approaching him, Esther carefully dodged the question by not complying until the following day. Vashti openly defied the king and publicly embarrassed him, but Esther hatched a more indirect plan by holding a private banquet and stroking the king's ego with flattery (see Esther 7:3-4). This deliberate strategy enabled Esther to triumph over the limitations placed upon her by her political and cultural situation. The passive young woman from chapter 2 has emerged as a bold and clever queen!

Conclusion

Although Vashti and Esther had limited power because of their patriarchal culture, the Old Testament remembers the ways in which they boldly challenged and subversively worked around it. These women demonstrate the ways in which God's people can faithfully remain resilient amidst cultural tensions. Their social context of subjugation and sexual abuse did not have the last say in God's story. Together, their actions remind God's people about the kingdom work God still is inviting us to do in our contexts, as we strive to live according to God's vision for mutual partnerships between men and women today.

CHRISTINA BOHN is assistant professor of Old Testament at MidAmerica Nazarene University. She is the co-author of *Genesis 12-50* in the *New Beacon Bible Commentary* series.

Unit 2

God in the Shadows

Session Outcome

To recognize that what is happening in our lives can be used by God to accomplish His purposes.

Customize:

Daniel is the password to access expanded teaching helps on FoundryLeader.com

 **Discover:**

Illustrated Bible Life takes us to the ancient city of Susa, and provides verse-by-verse commentary on the Scripture passage.

October

20

GOD WORKS BEHIND THE SCENES

Even when we cannot see it, God is working to accomplish His will in this world.

THE WORD

ESTHER 1:1-3

This is what happened during the time of Xerxes, the Xerxes who ruled over 127 provinces stretching from India to Cush: ²At that time King Xerxes reigned from his royal throne in the citadel of Susa, ³and in the third year of his reign he gave a banquet for all his nobles and officials. The military leaders of Persia and Media, the princes, and the nobles of the provinces were present.

10-12

¹⁰On the seventh day, when King Xerxes was in high spirits from wine, he commanded the seven eunuchs who served him—Mehuman, Biztha, Harbona, Bigtha, Abagtha, Zethar and Karkas—¹¹to bring before him Queen Vashti, wearing her royal crown, in order to display her beauty to the people and nobles, for she was lovely to look at. ¹²But when the attendants delivered the king's command, Queen Vashti refused to come. Then the king became furious and burned with anger.

ESTHER 2:1-2

¹Later when King Xerxes' fury had subsided, he remembered Vashti and what she had done and what he had decreed about her. ²Then the king's personal attendants proposed, "Let a search be made for beautiful young virgins for the king.

5-10

KEY VERSES

⁵Now there was in the citadel of Susa a Jew of the tribe of Benjamin, named Mordecai son of Jair, the son of Shimei, the son of Kish, ⁶who had been carried into exile from Jerusalem by Nebuchadnezzar king of Babylon, among those taken captive with Jehoiachin king of Judah. ⁷Mordecai had a cousin named

Last Week:

We saw how believers are to intercede on behalf of our faith communities for the good of God's kingdom.

This Week:

We will see that, despite our circumstances, God is at work to accomplish His will.

_____

_____

_____

_____

_____

_____

_____

_____

_____

_____

_____

_____

_____

_____

_____

_____

_____

_____

_____

_____

_____

Session 8

Hadassah, whom he had brought up because she had neither father nor mother. This young woman, who was also known as Esther, had a lovely figure and was beautiful. Mordecai had taken her as his own daughter when her father and mother died.

⁸When the king's order and edict had been proclaimed, many young women were brought to the citadel of Susa and put under the care of Hegai. Esther also was taken to the king's palace and entrusted to Hegai, who had charge of the harem. ⁹She pleased him and won his favor. Immediately he provided her with her beauty treatments and special food. He assigned to her seven female attendants selected from the king's palace and moved her and her attendants into the best place in the harem.

¹⁰Esther had not revealed her nationality and family background, because Mordecai had forbidden her to do so.

17   ¹⁷Now the king was attracted to Esther more than to any of the other women, and she won his favor and approval more than any of the other virgins. So he set a royal crown on her head and made her queen instead of Vashti.

ENGAGE THE WORD

A TIME WHEN PERSIANS RULED

Esther 1:1-3

The beginning of this story alerts the reader that the setting is during the reign of King Xerxes **(Heb. Ahasuerus),** a time when the Persians ruled over Judah. King Xerxes ruled from 486-465 BC. Esther 1:1 begins with the phrase "and it was in the days." This particular phrase is found in only four other places in the Old Testament: Genesis 14:1; Isaiah 7:1; Jeremiah 1:3; and Ruth 1:1. Most of the time this phrase is connected to a specific ruler, except in Ruth 1:1, which connects it to an era, "the days the judges ruled."

The opening scene also reveals a lavish banquet setting. Banquets (1:3, 5, 9; 2:18; 5:5; 7:1) and feasting (8:17; 9:17-22) are found throughout the story. Opulence is witnessed through references to cloth, clothing, and objects (see Esther 1:6-7), and are key items to pay attention to as they indicate shifts in power and markers of identity.

Watch:

Dr. Jim Edlin introduces this unit on Esther.

Listen:

FoundryLeader.com: This week's *Illustrated Bible Life* "Article Out Loud" journeys to the city of Susa, capital of the Persian Empire during the time of Esther.

Notes:

_____

_____

_____

_____

_____

_____

_____

_____

_____

_____

_____

_____

_____

_____

_____

_____

_____

Did You Know?

One of the main accounts outside of the biblical text that describes the context of Esther is from the writings of Herodotus, a Greek historian, who wrote extensively about King Xerxes in *Histories of the Persians Wars* (490-480 BC). His writings should be read with a healthy dose of skepticism because of his Greek allegiance, but it is intriguing that about a third of his book details the reign of King Xerxes.

HADASSAH

QUEEN VASHTI
Esther 1:10-12

Queen Vashti is hosting a banquet for the women while her husband is hosting a separate banquet. King Xerxes demands Queen Vashti to appear before him wearing her royal headdress/crown. Although there is some debate about what the entire request specifically entailed, the story records that she refuses to obey the order. After all, she was hosting her own banquet! Nevertheless, a king's command must be obeyed or dire consequences ensue for breaking the law.

After consultation with advisers, King Xerxes removes Vashti from her position as his queen and banishes her from his presence. Vashti's refusal to wear the crown will result in loss of power and rank, and an edict will be sent to all of the king's provinces that women should respect their husbands. The king's adviser, Memukan, might actually be in fear for his own household, as he worries for an uprising of "Persian women of nobility." Out of fear, an edict is sent to all of King Xerxes' provinces.

Esther 2:1-2, 5-10, 17

Although this part of the story has been misunderstood as a beauty contest for the next Queen of Persia, it is actually a scene where young women are taken against their wills. The edict that went out in chapter 1 will be mirrored in scope to request all the beautiful young virgins in all the provinces of Persia to be taken to the citadel of Susa.

The story now centers on the experience of a young Jewish woman, Hadassah (Heb. myrtle), who is also known as Esther (Persian: star). Esther is an orphan being raised by her cousin, Mordecai, in the citadel of Susa. Mordecai is from the tribe of Benjamin, whose family was exiled by the Babylonian king, Nebuchadnezzar. Esther is "beautiful" and has a "lovely figure." This description is also used of Jacob's wife, Rachel (Genesis 29:17) and Abigail, Nabal's wife (1 Samuel

Discover:

Through archaeological research and the reading of ancient texts, we can step back in time—through thousands of years in this case—to capture the history of one of the world's oldest cities and the backdrop for the Old Testament book of Esther: the ancient city of Susa. Let's explore "The Citadel of Susa" in this week's *Illustrated Bible Life* article.

Think About It

Vashti appears very briefly in the story of Esther. As the queen, she defies the king's order on the final day of the banquet. Rabbinic writers speculate that Vashti's refusal was due to the fact that she was requested to appear before the king with only her headdress/crown on and no clothes. Vashti's honor is never discussed, but her refusal makes a strong point. In a society with women's limited rights, Vashti takes a strong stand for herself and for women, losing her title, and her power as queen, and she could have risked her life as well. What is worth a risk in your life of faith?

25:3), who later becomes the wife of David. Esther is taken to be placed under the care of Hegai, to be given beauty treatments along with the other women. The women taken would all become concubines for the king, while one would be chosen for the position of the next queen. Aware of potential danger in revealing Esther's ethnic and religious identity, Esther obeys her cousin Mordecai and keeps her background a secret (2:10). The text reveals that Esther receives favor *(hesed)* from Hegai (2:9), and later favor from everyone (2:15), and finally, she gained favor and approval from the king (2:17). Esther will move from the house of the women to the king's house. King Xerxes will choose as his next queen, Esther, by placing the royal headdress upon her.

Though God appears hidden through this story, Esther has gained the favor of everyone she comes into contact with. Esther is experiencing something she has not chosen. In an ancient society where a woman's rights are limited or nonexistent, it is essential to recall the oppressiveness and loss of identity Esther experienced in her situation. Nevertheless, God is with Esther, even in the darkest moments of her life.

REFLECT Pray, asking God to open your eyes to His moving presence in your life.

JENNIFER MATHENY is former professor at Nazarene Theological Seminary and currently serves as associate professor of Christian Scriptures at George W. Truett Seminary—Baylor University.

Notes:

_____

_____

_____

_____

_____

_____

_____

_____

_____

_____

_____

_____

_____

_____

_____

_____

_____

_____

Discussion Guide

 Connect to My Experience

Suppose your Christian book club or Bible study group or this very class here today announces plans to study a book where God is never mentioned, not even a single time.

- Would you attend? Why or why not?

Today we begin a study of the book of Esther, where God is never mentioned.

- Why do you think the book of Esther was included in the canon of the Bible, considering there is no reference to God within the story?

- Why might God choose to keep His divine intervention active, but behind the scenes?

Transition:

Today we begin the story of Esther. Although she lived in an ancient culture and we are navigating a modern one, we can find similar ways to see God at work today.

Connect to the Word

Invite someone to read Esther 1:1-3, then discuss the following,

The setting is in the Persian Empire during the reign of King Xerxes [ZURK seez] the Great. The book of Esther documents what happened to some of the Jews who did not return to their homeland after the exile.

- What elements indicate that tremendous wealth and opulence were on display? Why might this be important to King Xerxes (see also 1:4-8)? (The extreme opulence and the duration [six months] of this parade of food, drink, and riches indicate Xerxes's tremendous pride.)

Invite someone to read Esther 1:10-12, then discuss the following,

On the 7th day of the party (v. 10), Xerxes decided that he wanted to put his wife on display along with his other riches. She was ordered to appear before his male guests, but she refused.

- How would you interpret the statement that King Xerxes was "in high spirits from wine"? (1:10) How do you think this might have eventually effected numerous lives? (His drunken actions effected Queen Vashti, all the virgins recruited to take her place, and all women throughout the empire.)

- Do you think Queen Vashti's refusal was justified? What was she risking by refusing? (She risked not only her crown, but her entire life.)

- How might Vashti's refusal mirror the plight of the Jews living counter-culturally in a secular society?

- Who do you think seems more prideful—Vashti or Xerxes? Why? Do you think these two showed lack of respect to the other? If so, how?

- How are pride and respect related? How can pride lead to unintended and detrimental outcomes that effect many lives? (Note that in 1:16-22, men became alarmed that Vashti's stand against her husband's commands could lead to wives everywhere doing the same. Edicts were issued throughout the kingdom making it not only custom but law that women respect their husbands and that men be the rulers of their households.)

Invite someone to read Esther 2:1-2, 5-10, and 17, then discuss the following,

The story shifts from King Xerxes to focus on two Jewish exiles who also lived in Susa: Mordecai [MAWR dih kigh] and Esther, who is also called Hadassah [huh DASS uh].

- What was the plan to find a new queen? (2:1-2) What does this further tell us about the role and value of women in this culture?

In verses 5-7 we learn about the lineage of Mordecai all the way back to the tribe of Benjamin, and consequently the lineage of Esther as well.

- Why is it important that we learn those details? (They are Jewish with a long lineage. Now they are exiles taken by force into a foreign land.)

- Why was it important that Esther's nationality and ethnicity not be revealed? (v. 10)

- Are there times when Christians should openly disclose matters of faith? (In "creative access" areas of the world, in situations where there is hostility toward believers, faith is shared less publicly.)

- Esther moved up in the parade of women to number 1. (2:8-9, 17) How do you think this happened? Was it her natural beauty (2:7)? The result of beauty treatments and special foods (2:9)? Was it a happy coincidence? Was she "destined" to be queen?

- Though God is not mentioned in these verses, how do you see the hidden hand of God at work in this situation?

 ## Connect to My Life and the World

Think about something that happened to you unexpectedly (i.e., job offer, financial gain, personal encounter with another).

- Do you believe this was mere chance? Destiny? Divinely orchestrated? Sometimes a coincidence? Do you believe in coincidences at all?

- Think about terrible circumstances that are blamed on God. How can we know whether to attribute credit to God or to circumstances?

- If God has ordained an unexpected and remarkable set of events to come together, and if we fail to recognize His intervention, to what are the results generally attributed? (If we credit an outcome to another person's intervention, luck, or our own abilities when God is the author, we fail to give Him the glory.)

- As a believer, how do you navigate the tension between holding your identity as one who is not a part of this world while still having to interact in this world? Where do you draw the line?

No one writes or sings lyrics that say, "God, be silent and hide your presence. Let us guess what you are doing." We sing songs and pray prayers for God to show us His glory, to show us His presence, to open the heavens so that we can see Him.

- When it seems God chooses to work anonymously with His "hidden hand," in what ways is it harder to discern His presence?

- What can you do in those times to recognize His silent or quieter involvement?

- What might God be trying to teach us in His hidden intervention?

Close with prayer.

Sessions 8-13 are written by Gay Leonard

Gay is a writer and avid traveler in retirement.

SESSION 9

Session Outcome

To be open and look for ways that God can use us right where we are in life.

Customize:

Daniel is the password to access expanded teaching helps on FoundryLeader.com

Discover:

Illustrated Bible Life takes a close look at the issue of human free will in contrast to the sovereignty of God, and provides verse-by-verse commentary on the Scripture passage.

Unit 2

God in the Shadows

October

27

ACCEPTING YOUR GOD-GIVEN ROLE

God gives each of us opportunity to decide if we will become part of His redemptive plan.

THE WORD

ESTHER 3:8-10

Then Haman said to King Xerxes, "There is a certain people dispersed among the peoples in all the provinces of your kingdom who keep themselves separate. Their customs are different from those of all other people, and they do not obey the king's laws; it is not in the king's best interest to tolerate them. ⁹If it pleases the king, let a decree be issued to destroy them, and I will give ten thousand talents of silver to the king's administrators for the royal treasury."

¹⁰So the king took his signet ring from his finger and gave it to Haman son of Hammedatha, the Agagite, the enemy of the Jews.

ESTHER 4:5-16

⁵Then Esther summoned Hathak, one of the king's eunuchs assigned to attend her, and ordered him to find out what was troubling Mordecai and why.

⁶So Hathak went out to Mordecai in the open square of the city in front of the king's gate. ⁷Mordecai told him everything that had happened to him, including the exact amount of money Haman had promised to pay into the royal treasury for the destruction of the Jews. ⁸He also gave him a copy of the text of the edict for their annihilation, which had been published in Susa, to show to Esther and explain it to her, and he told him to instruct her to go into the king's presence to beg for mercy and plead with him for her people.

⁹Hathak went back and reported to Esther what Mordecai had said. ¹⁰Then she instructed him to say to Mordecai, ¹¹"All the king's officials and the people of the royal provinces know that for any man or woman who approaches the king in the inner court without being summoned the king has but one law: that they be put to death unless

Last Week:

We learned that God is at work through the best and worst situations to accomplish His purposes.

This Week:

We will learn that we must be open to the ways God can work through us at any given time in our life.

the king extends the gold scepter to them and spares their lives. But thirty days have passed since I was called to go to the king."

¹²When Esther's words were reported to Mordecai, ¹³he sent back this answer: "Do not think that because you are in the king's house you alone of all the Jews will escape. ¹⁴For if you remain silent at this time, relief and deliverance for the Jews will arise from another place, but you and your father's family will perish. And who knows but that you have come to your royal position for such a time as this?"

KEY VERSES **¹⁵Then Esther sent this reply to Mordecai: ¹⁶"Go, gather together all the Jews who are in Susa, and fast for me. Do not eat or drink for three days, night or day. I and my attendants will fast as you do. When this is done, I will go to the king, even though it is against the law. And if I perish, I perish."**

ENGAGE THE WORD

In this portion of the Esther story, an important character enters the scene: Haman the Agagite. King Xerxes honors Haman and gives him "a seat of honor higher than all the others" (Esther 3:1). The insertion of Haman's background with its connection to the Amalekites (Agagites, descended from Agag, king of the Amalekites) reveals an important plot twist. That is, Esther is a queen whose Jewish identity is currently hidden and the king's right-hand man is an Amalekite, a group of people who hold animosity for the Jewish people (Exodus 17). In a moment during the king's public honor for Haman, Mordecai refuses to bow down to Haman. After questioning, the officials give a reason for Mordecai's refusal to bow down, because "he is a Jew" (Esther 3:4). Haman's position of power and influence enables him to take intentional and devious measures to address Mordecai's obstinance and use it as a tool for oppression for the entire Jewish population.

HAMAN'S PLOT **Esther 3:8-10**

Haman works a plot to twist partial truths to stir King Xerxes into action against an entire Jewish people. In Esther 1, Memukan's public discourse against

Notes:

🔊 **Listen:**

FoundryLeader.com: Why does God choose to "partner" with humans, and how does that work? These are some of the questions in this week's *Illustrated Bible Life* "Article Out Loud."

Notes:

_____

_____

_____

_____

_____

_____

_____

_____

_____

_____

_____

_____

_____

_____

_____

_____

Did You Know?
The book of Esther shares themes and similarities with many other books in the Christian canon. Esther and Ruth are the only two books named after women. Esther and Daniel share a similar storyline—both books detail life in exile and how the Jews flourish under foreign rule. Many themes parallel Joseph's life in Genesis, most notably in their difficult origin stories of loss and subsequent rise to power in a foreign land!

Vashti's actions result in a royal decree, meant to serve as warning for all wives (Esther 1:20). Similarly, Haman will levy one action of disrespect for possible annihilation of an entire people. Haman presents no solid confirmation that would warrant the king's decree, but Haman has learned how to manipulate the king and the king plays right into his hands. Haman advances the rhetoric that the Jews are different, disobedient, and keep themselves separate. Haman twists this to be a threat to the empire. Persian law allowed for diverse ethnic and religious groups to maintain adherence to their own laws. However, Haman finds a way to use this to incite the king's power and influence. He quickly offers a plan to remedy the problem to the narrative he has spun.

The king transfers a new power level to Haman as he removes the signet ring from his hand and bestows it into Haman's hand. Haman used this ring of power to send out a decree to all the king's provinces and in all the diverse languages of the Persian empire. Haman's intention is revealed in the edict and is absurdly disproportionate to Mordecai's actions. Haman commands a complete holocaust of the Jewish people. The decree commands people everywhere on the 13th day of the 12th month to destroy, to kill, and to annihilate every Jewish person, from young to the elderly.

MORDECAI MOURNS, ESTHER ACTS

Esther 4:5-16

Mordecai hears about the edict to destroy the Jewish people and changes his clothes into articles and elements of mourning: sackcloth and ashes (Esther 4:1-3). Esther hears about Mordecai mourning and, through her attendants, sends him a different set of clothes, but he refuses to put them on (Esther 3:4). This moment leads to Esther finding out about Haman's decree. Esther may be queen, but she is not privy to all the happenings around the province.

The knowledge of Esther's people on the verge of

Unit 2: God in the Shadows

🔍 Discover:

"God is in control." This is a phrase Christians often repeat, especially in times of trouble. It's a relief to know that when things are going off the rails, one can place one's trust in the Creator of the universe. At the same time, God often calls humans into partnership, to be God's co-workers in the task of caring for creation. What does this mean? This week's *Illustrated Bible Life* article, "Free Will Versus God's Sovereignty," explains.

Notes:

_____

Session 9

Think About It

Esther's origin story details her life as one of orphan raised by her cousin, Mordecai. The text does not go into detail about Esther's internal life, but it can be helpful to think about how she may have responded to possible danger as an adult after being a child who was orphaned. Esther may have desired to remain safe and hidden in the palace's protection after so much family loss. Do you think her origin story encouraged her bravery or made her boldness more difficult?

destruction becomes a moment of risk and possibility. Mordecai wisely asks, "And who knows but that you have come to your royal position for such a time as this?" (Esther 4:14b). Esther sends the message to Mordecai to call all Jews to fast and pray before she acts. Her identity as a Jewish woman has been hidden, but it is about to be revealed at possible peril. To approach the king unannounced can mean certain death. Esther's life hangs in the balance through one item of dress, the king's golden scepter. If it is extended to her, Esther will be able to approach the king. If not, she will be executed.

The transfer of an item of clothing is an important motif in the Esther story as it constructs and deconstructs power. In Esther 1, we see this movement with Queen Vashti's refusal to wear the headdress and her status moves from Queen Vashti (Esther 1:12) to Vashti (Esther 1:19). This headdress is placed upon Esther's head to "make her queen instead of Vashti" (Esther 2:17b). Here in Esther 3, the signet ring transfers from the hand of King Xerxes to Haman. The result of the power transfer is a decree that leaves the city of Susa confused and bewildered (Esther 3:15). Esther responds to the edict through a call for prayer and fasting. Although God is not mentioned in this story, God's hidden presence is revealed through the actions of God's people.

REFLECT Is there a current situation that might lead you to prayer and fasting?

JENNIFER MATHENY

Discussion Guide

Connect to My Experience

Begin your session by asking,

- What is a hate crime? ("Any of various crimes [such as assault or defacement of property] when motivated by hostility to the victim as a member of a group [such as one based on color, creed, gender, or sexual orientation]."–Merriam Webster)

- Why do you think we are seeing a rise in incidences of hate crimes?

- Why is a hate crime generally considered more heinous than others? (Innocent victims are chosen not specifically, but at random within a targeted group. Another name for hate crime is bias crime.)

- Have Christians and churches been the target of hate crimes? If so, how and why?

- Do you agree or disagree with this statement: "Bias toward other groups—expressed inwardly or outwardly-—is more prevalent today than we may want to admit." Why or why not?

Transition:

Today we will see that Haman hated the Jews as a group so much that he attempted the extinction of their entire race. God had a plan to prevent it through people who were willing to obey Him.

Connect to the Word

Invite someone to read Esther 3:8-10, then discuss the following,

Haman was an Agagite (3:1), a descendant of Agag, king of the Amalekites (1 Samuel 15:20). The Amalekites attacked the Israelites as they fled from Egyptian slavery, and King Agag later fought against Saul. This identifies Haman as an ancestral enemy of the Jews and helps to account for his hatred against all Jews. Haman had been recently elevated to a position higher than any other noble and received the honor that all the officials were to kneel before him (3:1-2).

- Why do you think Mordecai refused to bow down to Haman? (v. 3:2b) Was it because he bowed to no one but God (religious)? Was it because Haman was a descendant of the Amalekites, the enemy of the Jews since the days of the Exodus (racial, political)? Was it because Mordecai discerned Haman's character as undeserving of respect (personal)?

- With everyone else bowing in unity, why do you think Haman was so incensed over just one person not complying?

So great was Haman's anger that he sought to get rid not only of Mordecai, but all of Mordecai's race as well.

- What do you think accounts for this extreme overreaction? (pride, prejudice, hatred, history, insecurity)

Pride is a common theme in Esther. So, we see that Haman's response (mass murder of all Jews) to Mordecai's offence (disrespect) is ludicrously mismatched.

- Why is the emotion of pride so powerful? Which is more powerful—pride or wounded pride?

Haman not only proposed the extermination of an entire race, but he also promised the king 10,000 talents of silver (v. 9). Many believe Haman planned to plunder from the annihilated Jews' assets. Scholars believe greed of the Jews' riches was another motivation for Haman's plan to wipe them out of existence.

Insight

Israel and the Amalekites were fighting when Saul became king. Agag was the Amalekite king. Saul disobeyed God's command to kill Agag. Shortly after this, God would leave Saul and choose David to be the new king. Hundreds of years later, the children of Israel once again encountered the Amalekites in Persia. Mordecai and Haman continued the war that had started many years before either was born. When Haman found out Mordecai—the one man who would not bow down to him—was a Jew, he continued his ancestors' war and decided simple revenge was not enough. He would devise a plan to wipe out the Jewish race.

■ What does this indicate about the condition of Haman's heart?

Invite someone to read Esther 4:5-16, then discuss the following,

Mordecai learned what Haman had done and the king's edict. His response was to tear his clothes, put on sackcloth and ashes, and wail loudly outside the king's gate. Mordecai sends a message to Esther, asking her to approach the king and beg him for mercy for her people.

■ What would Esther risk by going to the king without being summoned? (v. 11)

■ Of what was Mordecai confident? (relief and deliverance for the Jews would come)

■ Does the responsibility for the Jewish race depend solely on Esther's involvement? If fear of her own death had caused her not to participate in the plan, would the Jews have been doomed to sure death? Why or why not? (v. 14)

Note that up until now Esther has seen no indication of any divine reason she was chosen as queen.

■ What does it mean that she had come to her royal position "for such a time as this"? (v. 14) Do you think this was just being at the right place at the right time, or something more? Explain.

Esther calls on the people to fast before she approaches the king.

■ What does this indicate about Esther's relationship with God?

■ Esther says she will go before the king regardless of the consequences (v. 16). What does this say about Esther's faith in God?

 ## Connect to My Life and the World

Esther—an orphan, a refugee, a woman in a patriarchal culture, a wife without choice—becomes the link to saving the entire Jewish race.

■ Do you consider Esther a hero? Why or why not?

■ Did she possess uncommon characteristics or abilities that enabled her to accept this assignment from God? Or, did she have characteristics that are common to all who accept God's help? What are those characteristics? (courage, commitment, sacrificial selflessness, dependence on God, fasting)

Share with your group: God uses individuals to accomplish His purposes. Whether they accept or refuse His invitation to participate, He will not abandon His plan. His deliverance lies within himself. He is faithful to make another way if necessary, but we will lose the blessing of participating in the victory.

If God is calling you to participate in His divine plan, do not wait for a smaller, a bigger, or a better role. Take courage from these words of Charles Spurgeon: "You have been wishing for another position where you could do something for Jesus: do not wish anything of the kind, but serve him where you are."

Close with a prayer of openness and consecration to trust God for deliverance and protection as we participate in God's daily leading this week.

SESSION 10

Session Outcome

To foster a belief that God can work His purposes in spite of people and circumstances that work against Him.

Customize:

Daniel is the password to access expanded teaching helps on FoundryLeader.com

Discover:

Illustrated Bible Life surveys ancient chronicles and libraries, and provides verse-by-verse commentary on the Scripture passage.

Unit 2

God in the Shadows

November

3

GOD HONORS HIS SERVANT

God surprises His people with honor and His enemies with justice.

THE WORD

ESTHER 5:11-14

Haman boasted to them about his vast wealth, his many sons, and all the ways the king had honored him and how he had elevated him above the other nobles and officials. ¹²"And that's not all," Haman added. "I'm the only person Queen Esther invited to accompany the king to the banquet she gave. And she has invited me along with the king tomorrow. ¹³But all this gives me no satisfaction as long as I see that Jew Mordecai sitting at the king's gate."

¹⁴His wife Zeresh and all his friends said to him, "Have a pole set up, reaching to a height of fifty cubits, and ask the king in the morning to have Mordecai impaled on it. Then go with the king to the banquet and enjoy yourself." This suggestion delighted Haman, and he had the pole set up.

ESTHER 6:1-10

¹That night the king could not sleep; so he ordered the book of the chronicles, the record of his reign, to be brought in and read to him. ²It was found recorded there that Mordecai had exposed Bigthana and Teresh, two of the king's officers who guarded the doorway, who had conspired to assassinate King Xerxes.

³"What honor and recognition has Mordecai received for this?" the king asked.

"Nothing has been done for him," his attendants answered.

⁴The king said, "Who is in the court?" Now Haman had just entered the outer court of the palace to speak to the king about impaling Mordecai on the pole he had set up for him.

⁵His attendants answered, "Haman is standing in the court."

"Bring him in," the king ordered.

Last Week:

We discovered the way believers must choose whether or not to be open to God to use them for His glory.

This Week:

We will discover the way God works His purposes despite those who work against Him.

⁶When Haman entered, the king asked him, "What should be done for the man the king delights to honor?"

Now Haman thought to himself, "Who is there that the king would rather honor than me?" ⁷So he answered the king, "For the man the king delights to honor, ⁸have them bring a royal robe the king has worn and a horse the king has ridden, one with a royal crest placed on its head. ⁹Then let the robe and horse be entrusted to one of the king's most noble princes. Let them robe the man the king delights to honor, and lead him on the horse through the city streets, proclaiming before him, 'This is what is done for the man the king delights to honor!'"

KEY VERSE

¹⁰"Go at once," the king commanded Haman. "Get the robe and the horse and do just as you have suggested for Mordecai the Jew, who sits at the king's gate. Do not neglect anything you have recommended."

ENGAGE THE WORD

Esther 5 marks a key scene and turning point for Esther. Esther puts on her royalty and stands in the inner court of the palace, ready to enter the king's hall. Here, the text calls her Esther (Esther 5:1), but once she changes into her royal robes, she becomes "Queen Esther" (Esther 5:2). In this moment she stands on behalf of all of her people.

The king favors Esther and he extends his golden scepter. This movement indicates life and hope, not only for Esther, but all of the Jewish people. The king has so much favor for Esther that he asks her request and he offers up to half of his kingdom! Wisdom is revealed through Esther as she carefully navigates this generous offer.

HAMAN'S ARROGANCE

Esther 5:11-14

Haman's pride comes on full display as he brags about his invitation to the banquet Esther has prepared for him and the king. He brags about his wealth, his position, and his power to his family. He also had a run in with Mordecai earlier and, fueled with rage, erects poles to have Mordecai impaled upon. Haman

Notes:

Listen:

FoundryLeader.com: Record-keeping in the ancient Near East is the focus in this week's *Illustrated Bible Life* "Article Out Loud."

Notes:

_____

_____

_____

_____

_____

_____

_____

_____

_____

_____

_____

_____

_____

_____

_____

Did You Know?
Cloth and clothing in Esther are presented to the limits of excess. Reading with an eye towards extravagance adds to this court narrative's literary beauty and complexity. Language of opulence through clothing is seen through 12 key scenes with important characters including Xerxes, Vashti, Esther, Mordecai, and Haman (1:6; 1:11; 2:17; 3:12; 4:1-4; 4:11; 5:1; 5:2; 6:6-11; 8:2; 8:4; 8:15).

UNEXPECTED HONOREE

is infuriated that Mordecai did not rise in this scene (Esther 5:9). Literary irony is at play in Esther 5, as Mordecai neither bows (3:2) nor rises (5:9) before Haman to show respect. Haman's mind is obsessed with Mordecai's irreverence for him. The violence in his heart for Mordecai and the Jewish people become publicly visible as he erects this immense pole, 50 cubits high (around 75 feet)! Haman is intensely focused on the one thing he cannot have or control. Obsessive ruminations can make one miss out on the many good things all around.

Esther 6:1-10

Even though God is not overtly named in the story, it becomes clear that God orchestrates justice and honor in surprising an unforeseen ways. In Esther 6, honor comes into the fore and full circle in this chapter. In chapter 1, the king's honor is a key theme in the decree given after Vashti's act of refusal to come before the king in her headdress/crown. We also see this in Memukan's concern for the king's honor (Esther 1:20) and even his greatness. Honor continues to resurface here in the narrative, as well as, irony and reversals.

The king cannot sleep and requests for the book of annals to be read to him, perhaps in hopes this will calm his mind to sleep. Here we also see the providence of God come into play . . . for a king and his attendants focused on honor, one of the stories read is about Mordecai! Mordecai averted an assassination plot against the king and was never honored! Haman is summoned to help the king out with this quandary. Haman's pride is glaring in this moment. The king asks Haman what he should do for "a man the king desires to honor" (Esther 6:6). Haman immediately hears honor and assumes the king is talking about him! Haman is all about Haman. This phrase, "the man the king desires to honor" is referred to three times in this chapter (Esther 6:6, 7, 9). Oh the irony of who deserves honor!

Discover:

When King Xerxes of Persia couldn't sleep one night, he called on one of his attendants to read to him from "the book of the chronicles" (Esther 6:1). It turns out this is not the only such ancient record mentioned in Scripture. What was this book, and what other chronicles and writings appear in our Bibles? Find out in this week's *Illustrated Bible Life* article, "Record-Keeping by Ancient Kingdoms."

Notes:

Session 10

Think About It

The story of Esther, the story of Joseph (Genesis 37—50), and Daniel 1—6, share important characteristics. These stories have been called court narratives, a common genre of writing in the ancient Near East context. Reading them together can be fascinating as they each detail life under a foreign ruler and seek to illustrate diverse ways to live out the complexities of a life of faith and loyalty to God under difficult circumstances.

Haman presents an extravagant plan to honor this "one the king desires to honor." Haman imagines that there is no one else in the entire Persian provinces that deserves honor more than himself (Esther 6:6b)!

The clothing motif plays into the irony of reversals in the following scenes. Haman suggests a change of clothes for this honored one, the kings royal robes. The "royal crest" on the horse is the royal headdress or crown. This headdress reminds the reader of the one worn by Vashti and Esther (Esther 1:11; 2:17) and the royal robes Esther places on herself before she courageously stood before the king in the inner court (Esther 5:1). To Haman's dismay, his elaborate suggestions will result in honor displayed with royal robes upon Mordecai, a royal headdress on the horse, and Haman himself parading his enemy, Mordecai, around Susa! (Clearly, and ironically, Haman's request for a horse the king has ridden reveals his ambitions.)

This kingly moment turns dramatically as Haman hears the honoree named: Mordecai. The reversals Haman begins to experience he shares with his family. His celebratory mood changes to a "head covered in grief" (Esther 6:12) as he joins the king at the second banquet Esther has prepared.

REFLECT Do not take revenge, my dear friends, but leave room for God's wrath, for it is written: 'It is mine to avenge; I will repay,' says the Lord" (Romans 12:19).

JENNIFER MATHENY

Discussion Guide

Connect to My Experience

Imagine or think of an actual conflict situation with an employer, teacher, law enforcement officer, or other authority figure. You feel strongly that you are in the right, but you lack the credentials or ability to make your case. Consider who you would turn for help to intervene on your behalf.

- What does it mean to intervene?

- How does the process of intervening differ from interfering? Is there a proper time and way to intervene?

- What are the qualities needed for someone to intervene effectively?

- What is involved in the following:
  —a medical intervention
  —an addiction intervention
  —a prayer intervention

- In what ways does God use intervention in His dealings with humanity?

- In what ways are we called to intervene for others?

Transition:

Throughout the Bible we see God's divine intervention. God will not forsake us. He shows His nature in the story of Esther to bring about good for His people.

Connect to the Word

Invite someone to read Esther 5:11-14, then discuss the following,

King Xerxes and Haman have been invited to a second banquet. Haman is happy until he sees his enemy Mordecai. Although he is filled with rage, he restrains himself, goes home, and surrounds himself with his wife and friends.

- What accomplishments and honors does Haman boast about? (5:11-12) Why do you think it was important to him to detail this list to his wife and family?

- Despite all his boasting, Haman cannot find peace. What irrational obsession causes him to be tragically conflicted within? (5:13) What does this tell us about Haman's character?

Invite someone to read Esther 6:1-10, then discuss the following,

When the king couldn't sleep that night, he asked that the record of his reign be brought in and read to him. When the plot to assassinate Xerxes was read to him, Xerxes asked how Mordecai had been rewarded for saving His life, and discovered that he had not.

- How did Xerxes learn that Mordecai's previous actions had saved his life? (6:1-2)

- How is it possible that out of all the chronicles in the royal library with all of the history recorded, the passage chosen by Xerxes's attendant would be about Mordecai? Is this coincidence? Ordained by God? The intervention of a divinely guided attendant who chose the specific book and the exact page? (Whether God intervenes through other people or through divine measures of His own, this was extremely exact in delivery. God is at work.)

- Why does the king employ Haman in determining what would constitute worthy recognition for the "man the king delights to honor"? ([v. 6] Haman was his top advisor.) Why does Haman presumptively assume that man is him?

Haman might be considered an "egomaniac": obsessively conceited, self-absorbed, arrogant, interested only in what benefits oneself, exaggerated sense of one's own abilities, exaggerated sense of importance, and an inability to empathize with the plight of others.

Insight

No simple death sentence would satisfy Haman's unbounded rage. He chose one of the most cruel, violent, and gruesome methods of execution: impalement. In vertical impalement, the victim was placed upright on a tall pole (in this case 75 feet tall) on a pointed stake and pulled down by his legs through his entire body until the stake protruded through his neck. Even with the extermination of the Jewish race already scheduled, this is the level of Haman's vengeance against a single man, Mordecai.

■ Discuss the ways Haman suggests the king honor the man he wishes to honor. (6:7-9)

The words of Jesus never ring truer than in this moment: "For whoever exalts himself will be humbled, and whoever humbles himself will be exalted" (Matthew 23:12).

■ In what way was public humiliation the consequence for Haman's self-centeredness?

■ How have you seen a person's out-of-control ego lead him/her to experience (unintended) negative consequences?

■ Read each statement below, pausing to reflect on the way God intervened:

—Mordecai would get the honor he deserved.

—Haman got the disgrace he deserved.

—Haman's impalement plans were thwarted.

—Mordecai's life was spared.

—Haman's influence among the people would be damaged.

—The Jews were one step closer to being saved from extermination.

Connect to My Life and the World

In the rain forest, there is a tree called the Strangler Fig. Its tiny seeds are indigestible to birds, who drop them in the top of mighty trees of the rain forest. The seeds germinate and send out vines that coil around the tree toward the ground, where they eventually penetrate the earth and take root. The leaves of the vine rob the host tree of sun, and the roots rob it of moisture and nutrients. Eventually the host tree is fully surrounded, dies, and decays, leaving a hollow shaft where a mighty tree once stood.

■ What were the tiny seeds that grew into a strangler and brought about the downfall of Haman?

■ What other seeds are there that are capable of destroying even the mighty people of God? (e.g., envy, bitterness, anger, jealousy, covetousness, and so on)

■ How do we guard against these strangler seeds, such as pride?

We see many in today's story seeking and/or receiving counsel.

■ To whom did these people go for counsel?
—Xerxes (Haman)
—Haman (Zeresh and his friends)
—Esther (Mordecai and God through fasting)

■ What is the danger of surrounding yourself with only those who think like you or will tell you only what they know will please you?

■ In what way does pride keep us from asking for godly advice? Why should we all, at at certain times, seek guidance?

■ What are the characteristics of a person from whom you should seek advice?

■ What are important steps to seeking counsel from God?

Close with a prayer.

Session Outcome

To follow God's wisdom in dealing with adversaries of God's kingdom.

Customize:

Daniel is the password to access expanded teaching helps on FoundryLeader.com

Discover:

Illustrated Bible Life explores the seeming absence of God in the book of Esther, and gives verse-by-verse commentary on the Scripture passage.

Unit 2

God in the Shadows

November

10

A DISCERNING QUEEN

God gives wisdom to His faithful as they fight against the evil of this world.

THE WORD

ESTHER 5:1-5

On the third day Esther put on her royal robes and stood in the inner court of the palace, in front of the king's hall. The king was sitting on his royal throne in the hall, facing the entrance. ² When he saw Queen Esther standing in the court, he was pleased with her and held out to her the gold scepter that was in his hand. So Esther approached and touched the tip of the scepter.

³Then the king asked, "What is it, Queen Esther? What is your request? Even up to half the kingdom, it will be given you."

⁴"If it pleases the king," replied Esther, "let the king, together with Haman, come today to a banquet I have prepared for him."

⁵"Bring Haman at once," the king said, "so that we may do what Esther asks."

So the king and Haman went to the banquet Esther had prepared.

ESTHER 7:1-6

¹So the king and Haman went to Queen Esther's banquet, ²and as they were drinking wine on the second day, the king again asked, "Queen Esther, what is your petition? It will be given you. What is your request? Even up to half the kingdom, it will be granted."

KEY VERSE

³**Then Queen Esther answered, "If I have found favor with you, Your Majesty, and if it pleases you, grant me my life—this is my petition. And spare my people—this is my request.** ⁴For I and my people have been sold to be destroyed, killed and annihilated. If we had merely been sold as male and female slaves, I would have kept quiet, because no such distress would justify disturbing the king."

⁵King Xerxes asked Queen Esther, "Who is he? Where is he—the man who has dared to do such a thing?"

Last Week:

We gained a deeper understanding of how both goodness and wickedness eventually receive their just rewards.

This Week:

We will gain a deeper understanding of how God gives discernment to His faithful people.

⁶Esther said, "An adversary and enemy! This vile Haman!" Then Haman was terrified before the king and queen.

9-10

⁹Then Harbona, one of the eunuchs attending the king, said, "A pole reaching to a height of fifty cubits stands by Haman's house. He had it set up for Mordecai, who spoke up to help the king."
The king said, "Impale him on it!" ¹⁰So they impaled Haman on the pole he had set up for Mordecai. Then the king's fury subsided.

ENGAGE THE WORD

A WOMAN OF PRAYER AND COURAGE

Esther 5:1-5

Esther didn't abandon her people—she stood up for them, identified herself with them, and took action on their behalf. As a woman in Persian society, Esther had very little power and few individual rights. By virtue of her position as queen, she had some influence.

Esther is a woman of prayer and courage. In Esther 5, Esther immediately calls for prayer and fasting when she hears about the decree to annihilate her people. After three days, she dresses in her royal robes and approaches the king. Receiving his favor, Esther wisely sets up a series of banquets before she makes her formal request. Between these two banquets, a turn of events has occurred with the honoring of Mordecai.

In a seemingly hopeless situation, God has been at work. This is a reminder to hope and pray against the visible/material (and spiritual) forces that are opposed to God's people. Even when there appears to be no way through a difficult or even oppressive situation, God creatively acts through unconventional means, like a king's insomnia (6:1).

ESTHER'S REQUEST

Esther 7:1-6, 9-10

Esther's second banquet mirrors the first. The question from the king remains the same, "Queen Esther, what is your petition? It will be given you. What is your request? Even up to half the kingdom, it will be granted" (Esther 7:2). Similar to Esther 5:3, the king refers

🔊 **Listen:**

FoundryLeader.com: Why does the book of Esther never mention God's name? That's the question in this week's *Illustrated Bible Life* "Article Out Loud."

Notes:

_____

_____

_____

_____

_____

_____

_____

_____

_____

_____

_____

_____

_____

_____

_____

_____

Did You Know?

One of the disturbing moments in the Esther story is when Haman devises a scheme to destroy the Jewish people and King Xerxes gives Haman the power to go forth with his plan without ever seeking out details about who these particular people are in his kingdom (Esther 3:1-11). King Xerxes is portrayed as a leader who can be swayed, is self-indulgent, and fueled by his carnal desires. Fortunately, the tales of reversal will turn in favor of God's people and God will use Esther to turn the motivation of this king in their favor.

to Esther as "Queen Esther." In this moment, Esther is ready to boldly make the request. Esther addresses the king respectfully and with honor. In this request, Esther will add to it a request for her life and for the life of her people to be spared. Using the language of servitude, Esther says that she and her people have been sold to be completely wiped out (7:4).

Haman's initial approach to the king in Esther 3 was an attractive offer...weaving a tale of profit and honor to gain the king's favor in issuing the edict against the Jewish people. Esther repurposes similar language that Haman used in Esther 3. Esther says, "For I and my people have been sold to be destroyed, killed and annihilated. If we had merely been sold as male and female slaves, I would have kept quiet, because no such distress would justify disturbing the king" (Esther 7:4). The language used here of being "sold" brings up intertextual allusion to the story of Joseph being sold by his brothers in Genesis 37:28, 36, and 45:4.

King Xerxes takes in all Esther has spoken and is rightly enraged. He immediately asks who has threatened his queen and her people. Esther responds, "An adversary and enemy! This vile Haman!" The writer has already indicated in Esther 3 that Haman is the "foe/enemy" of the Jews. Here, at this moment in time, Haman is not only the enemy of the Jews, but he is also Esther's enemy and the king's! The king recuses himself to the garden in his anger. Haman stays behind with Esther to plead for his life.

Haman "stands" in this scene to plead for Esther to save his life. Before the king returns, Haman is lying prostrate before Esther. Upon the king's return, he sees Haman lying near Esther and the king accuses Haman of sexually advancing upon the queen while the king is "in the house." Some scholars wonder if perhaps the king accuses Haman of this inappropriate posture to have a reason to punish him immediately. This moment is the apex of irony, a scene filled with Haman being dishonored. The Hebrew text states that

Discover:

Why would the Bible, the written Word of God, contain a book that never mentions God's name? The book of Esther contains about 5,600 Hebrew words, but not one direct reference to God by name or even indirectly by a pronoun. Let's take a closer look at "God in the Book of Esther" in this week's *Illustrated Bible Life* article.

Notes:

Think About It

Esther displays strong connections to wisdom literature. In wisdom literature, groups of people can be seen as "types" or "typecast," such as "the wicked" and "the righteous." If you begin to read Proverbs, these "types" become evident very quickly. The story of Job provides a helpful counterbalance to an overly simplified typecast of individuals. Reading books like these together is important to encompass a broader and more complex outlook on life and theology.

Haman is accused of conquering the queen. What a plot twist! Haman has tried to conquer, to destroy the Jews. In a swift turn of events, Haman will be impaled on the pole he built for Mordecai.

This final scene brings a close to the animosity between Mordecai and Haman. The narrative brilliantly uses confusion and misinterpretation of events to raise the level of irony and humor. In chapter 6, Haman misunderstands who the king desires to honor. Here in chapter 7, the king misinterprets (intentionally?) Haman's posture before Esther. Adele Berlin writes, "The irony is that now both Esther and Ahasuerus have accused Haman of gross insubordination–of wishing to supplant the king . . .Haman's lust for honor has at last been laid bare, and it proves his undoing."[1]

1. Adele Berlin. *Esther: THE JPS Bible Commentary* (Philadelphia: Jewish Publication Society, 2001), 64-65.

REFLECT In what ways can you intercede on behalf of those who are facing injustice?

JENNIFER MATHENY

Discussion Guide

Connect to My Experience

Each culture has its own idioms to express falling victim to one's own schemes meant to harm another. Finish these phrases:

—You made your own bed _____ (now lie in it).

—You reap what you _____ (sow).

—You dug your own grave _____ (now lie in it).

—Now you get a taste of your own _____ (medicine).

—"If a man digs a pit, he will fall into it; if a man rolls a stone, it will _____ (roll back on him)."—Proverbs 26:27

—What goes around _____ (comes around).

—If you live by the sword _____ (you will die by the sword).

◼ Why do you think these idioms/proverbs are universal truths? Is there a fundamental moral basis for this?

Transition:

Today we will see how Haman experienced this kind of truism as a result of his evil plans against the Jews.

Connect to the Word

Invite someone to read Esther 5:1-5, then discuss the following,

King Xerxes asked again what he could do for Esther. She requested that he and Haman come to a banquet. At that time, she would make her request of the king.

◼ Why do you think she invited Haman as the only other guest? (It was a strategic move for Haman's wickedness to be exposed before the king.)

◼ Esther asked them to attend a second banquet (5:8). What can we learn from her actions? (Don't rush forward when you sense that God is saying to wait. Follow the Spirit. Exercise wisdom and patience.)

Invite someone to read Esther 7:1-6, then discuss the following,

The king asks Esther what her petition is. He says that he would offer "up to half the kingdom" to her. This was a proverbial expression, stressing his great respect, admiration, and perhaps even genuine love for Queen Esther.

◼ Why do you think Esther was granted such extreme favor with the king, far beyond what Xerxes had for Vashti and perhaps more than a king normally has for any queen?

◼ Here is the critical moment. What are all the unknowns about to be revealed? Who is about to find out something he/she did not know?

—Esther will find out if her life and the Jewish people will be spared.

—The king will discover that the people group Haman asked permission to kill is the Jewish race. (Previously the king failed to ask, and Haman discreetly failed to tell.)

—The king will discover that Esther is a Jew and that Haman is plotting the death not only of all the Jews, but of the queen as well.

—Haman will know for the first time that the queen is Jewish and that he has asked to kill the king's own wife and all her people.

◼ Why do you think Esther uses slavery language ("sold") for their death? (7:4) (Haman would have indeed profited from the death of all the Jews. He possibly intended to confiscate all their wealth [3:11].)

Insight

Immediately upon being identified by Esther as "the adversary and enemy," Haman knew his fate was sealed and was terrified. "As soon as the word left the king's mouth, they covered Haman's face" (7:8). Persians covered the face of anyone who angered the king so that he might never see his face again. Greeks and Romans also covered the faces of the condemned. When a Roman judge condemned a criminal, his head was immediately covered, and he was sent to die.

Invite someone to read Esther 7:9-10, then discuss the following,

King Xerxes had to ask, "Who has dared to do such a thing?" (7:5).

- Why do you think the king was unaware of who Esther was talking about considering his encounter with Haman in 3:8-10? (He was blinded power and the mistreatment of other people groups.)

Like a sentenced man digging his own grave, Haman had constructed his own instrument of death, and it was ready immediately.

- What is the sad irony at this point in the story? (Haman constructed an instrument of death for Mordecai; instead, it was an instrument of death for him.)
- Share a time when you saw this type of irony played out in your, or someone else's, life.

Jesus said that His kingdom is upside down to the world (i.e., the first is last, the greatest is least).

- How was Haman's life completely upside down? (he sought honor but was disgraced; meant to kill Mordecai but was killed himself, etc.)
- What lesson can we learn from the end of Haman's tragic life?

Connect to My Life and the World

Ask group members to write their own idioms/proverbs for Haman by completing the statement below.

"He who builds a 75-foot impalement pole _____."

- Why do you think God allows evil people to gain power politically, economically, culturally, or within a family or organization?
- How can Christians respond when evil exists in the world on such a great scale?

On a scale of 1-10—with 1 being not at all and 10 being very much so—how would you compare yourself to these characteristics Esther possessed?

- **Hope.** Esther maintained her hope that God would protect her life as she went to the king without invitation, that she would find favor, and that her people would be saved. In what do you place your hope? When situations look bleak, how do you find hope?
- **Courage/Bravery.** Esther risked her own life, as well as the lives of all her people. Rarely are we called to save someone's life, but frequently we are called to stand for others when they cannot stand for themselves. What does this look like for you?
- **Defiance.** Although Esther was queen, she was also a woman in a patriarchal society where women had no rights. Yet, she stood up to the men in her life when needed. Sometimes we are called to holy defiance against evil. How do you square this with the humility of a Christian?
- **Leadership.** Esther accepted her role of leadership not only as queen, but as a Jew. How do you need to step up in leadership in your home, school, workplace, or church?

Close in prayer.

Session Outcome

To cooperate with God to bring about the deliverance that God brings to His people.

Customize:

Daniel is the password to access expanded teaching helps on FoundryLeader.com

Discover:

Illustrated Bible Life looks at Haman's deep hatred of Mordecai and his people, and provides verse-by-verse commentary on the Scripture passage.

Unit 2

God in the Shadows

November

17

GOD DELIVERS HIS PEOPLE

God makes a way for His people to overcome the enemies of His kingdom.

THE WORD

ESTHER 8:3-13

Esther again pleaded with the king, falling at his feet and weeping. She begged him to put an end to the evil plan of Haman the Agagite, which he had devised against the Jews. ⁴Then the king extended the gold scepter to Esther and she arose and stood before him.

⁵"If it pleases the king," she said, "and if he regards me with favor and thinks it the right thing to do, and if he is pleased with me, let an order be written overruling the dispatches that Haman son of Hammedatha, the Agagite, devised and wrote to destroy the Jews in all the king's provinces. ⁶For how can I bear to see disaster fall on my people? How can I bear to see the destruction of my family?"

⁷King Xerxes replied to Queen Esther and to Mordecai the Jew, "Because Haman attacked the Jews, I have given his estate to Esther, and they have impaled him on the pole he set up. ⁸Now write another decree in the king's name in behalf of the Jews as seems best to you, and seal it with the king's signet ring—for no document written in the king's name and sealed with his ring can be revoked."

⁹At once the royal secretaries were summoned—on the twenty-third day of the third month, the month of Sivan. They wrote out all Mordecai's orders to the Jews, and to the satraps, governors and nobles of the 127 provinces stretching from India to Cush. These orders were written in the script of each province and the language of each people and also to the Jews in their own script and language. ¹⁰Mordecai wrote in the name of King Xerxes, sealed the dispatches with the king's signet ring, and sent them by mounted couriers, who rode fast horses especially bred for the king.

¹¹The king's edict granted the Jews in every city the right to

Last Week:

We explored our need to trust God's wisdom and patiently rely on His justice.

This Week:

We will explore our need to cooperate with God in the deliverance He offers to people.

assemble and protect themselves; to destroy, kill and annihilate the armed men of any nationality or province who might attack them and their women and children, and to plunder the property of their enemies. [12]The day appointed for the Jews to do this in all the provinces of King Xerxes was the thirteenth day of the twelfth month, the month of Adar. **[13]A copy of the text of the edict was to be issued as law in every province and made known to the people of every nationality so that the Jews would be ready on that day to avenge themselves on their enemies.**

KEY VERSE

ENGAGE THE WORD

REVERSALS

Esther 8:3-13

Esther's courage and agency to plead for her people continues in this chapter. Her personal world was safe. She could have accepted the gift of Haman's property for her family and allowed herself to be insulated in the safety of the palace in Susa. Instead, Esther risks her life for her people. Because the king gave the edict, it could not be revoked. Esther now brings her cousin Mordecai before the king. Together, this unsuspecting Jewish family will now have power and influence, even in exile. The ways of God are profound! King Xerxes gives Mordecai his signet ring. What a reversal! Originally on Haman's hand, now Mordecai has charge over Haman's estate and the signet ring. The theme of reversals is woven all throughout Esther 8.

Scholars demonstrate the literary artistry of the book of Esther. In chapter 8, language is reused for emphasis and many phrases are parallel to chapter 3. Here are a few examples of reversals and repetition:

- The repeated phrase: "Haman, the 'enemy' of the Jews" (3:10; 8:1)
- Mordecai is given Haman's property and Mordecai is brought before the king, like Haman (3:1; 8:1-2).
- The king's signet ring is given to Haman (3:10). The king's signet ring is given to Mordecai (8:2)
- An edict is given to destroy the Jews (3:13-15). An edict is given to allow the Jews to defend themselves (8:11)

Notes:

_____

_____

_____

_____

_____

_____

_____

_____

_____

_____

_____

_____

_____

_____

_____

_____

 **Listen:**

FoundryLeader.com: This week's *Illustrated Bible Life* "Article Out Loud" explains what may have motivated Haman's intense hatred of the Jewish people.

Notes:

_____

_____

_____

_____

_____

_____

_____

_____

_____

_____

_____

_____

_____

_____

_____

_____

_____

_____

Did You Know?

Esther is part of a group of scrolls in Jewish tradition called the *Megillot* (five scrolls). This group of scrolls include Ruth, Lamentations, Song of Songs, and Ecclesiastes (Qohelet). In the Tiberian ordering of books, these five scrolls begin with Ruth and ends with Esther (Ruth, Songs, Qohelet, Lamentations, Esther). Each scroll connects to one of the five major holidays of the Jewish liturgical year.

• The people of Susa are bewildered at the edict (3:15). The Jews of Susa rejoice at the new edict (8:17).

The language of both edicts is violent. In the first edict in Esther 3, the instructions are to destroy, to kill, and to annihilate every Jewish person, including women and children! Here in Esther 8, literary reversals are seen in the new edict. The Jewish people are given power to destroy, to kill, and to annihilate those who attack the Jews.

Because the old edict could not be reversed, the Jews could legally protect themselves in this dark hour. Some of the language is different than the first in the second edict. Mordecai's instructions call for the Jewish people to "assemble" and to "protect" themselves. In the Hebrew this is "to stand for their lives." What is also notable is that unlike the first edict that calls for the people of Persia to attack the Jews; here, the Jewish people are to attack the "armed forces" that are coming against them. The language indicates agency for the Jews to defend themselves. The harsh language of the second edict parallels the first and is meant to match the intensity of attack with intensity to defend. The edict is quickly sent on the 23rd day of Sivan, the third month. There are less than 9 months to get the word out.

When Esther is read, the focus is often on Esther's rise to power and the personal risk she took to save the Jewish people. Reading through this story more slowly, it becomes evident that there is much violence in this story. This can be one of the difficult realities when reading the Old Testament. It is helpful to remember that these are very ancient stories within an ancient Near Eastern context. One helpful reading strategy is to step back and think about where God has worked through the lives of people and individuals in very difficult situations.

In Esther 9:17b it states that, "And many people of other nationalities became Jews because fear of the

Discover:

Vain, vindictive, vile, and vicious are but a few of the adjectives justly applied to the Babylonian ruler's chief minister, who nearly succeeded in destroying an entire people. What prompted Haman? Why did he hate Mordecai and his fellow Jews so deeply? Let's find out in this week's *Illustrated Bible Life* article, "Why Did Haman Hate the Jewish People?"

Notes:

_____

_____

_____

_____

_____

_____

_____

_____

_____

_____

_____

_____

_____

_____

_____

_____

_____

_____

_____

Session 12

Think About It

Thinking about Esther as part of a group of scrolls celebrated through the Jewish liturgical year, it becomes apparent that theology is embodied through practices which include reading, singing, celebration, and even fasting. Michael LeFebvre writes that festivals do not serve the "chronology of history but the cadence of worship."[1] What are important rhythms for you in the Christian calendar year that inspire you to live out your theology in community? What are key practices (e.g., celebrations, fasting, worship) that you find meaningful?

Jews had seized them." This verse has been a source of scholarly discussion as you might imagine. Was there conversion out of fear? This does not resonate well with our modern care and commitment to evangelism! In the Hebrew, the non-Jewish people are referred to as "people of the land." One translation states that this could be "they identified themselves with the Jews" (Levenson) or "sided with the Jews" (Berlin). So rather than conversion, this verse could mean that the people of the land took the side of the Jews and defended them against their attackers. This is not to say that there were not converts to Judaism. We see this all throughout the Old Testament.

God's heart desires peace and care for our neighbors. The reality is that this is not always lived out. Haman sought to destroy God's people and issued an edict that could not be reversed. Recalling Esther's rise to power, she risked violence upon herself to save her people. Risking the life of one to save a group is the heart of sacrifice and love for neighbor. Haman authored a death notice for the Jews. Esther and Mordecai found a way to protect the lives of the Jewish people. God makes a way for His people to overcome the enemies of God's kingdom!

1. Michael LeFebvre. *The Liturgy of Creation* (Westmont: IVP Academic, 2019), 93.

REFLECT In what ways have you seen God's protection in the lives of His faithful followers?

JENNIFER MATHENY

Discussion Guide

Connect to My Experience

Begin your session by asking your group,

- What do "revocable" and "irrevocable" mean?

- Name an example of agreements in everyday life that are revocable or irrevocable. (*Revocable:* Cancelling a flight reservation where allowed. A driver's license is revocable upon certain infractions by the driver. *Irrevocable:* Returning purchased items that have been used, damaged, or in any way violate the store's policy. Human rights are irrevocable.)

Transition:

Today, we look at Esther's influence to save her people despite an irrevocable decree of the king.

Connect to the Word

Invite someone to read Esther 8:3-8, then discuss the following,

The first edict sent to all 127 provinces of the Persian Empire declared that all Jews were to be herded together and slaughtered on the same day. The edict was irrevocable. That is why Esther was weeping and pleading with King Xerxes after the death of Haman (8:3). The evil that had been set in motion against the Jews was still to take place.

- How did the king honor Esther and Mordecai after Haman's death? ([8:1-2] They were not only safe; they were also elevated in power and wealth.)

Though Haman was now dead and Esther and Mordecai were safe, "the evil plan of Haman the Agagite" lived on (8:3).

- Why were all the Jews living across the Persian Empire not yet safe? (It was an irrevocable edict of the king.)

- How does Esther once again risk her life to intervene before the king for the safety of her people? (8:5) Each time she went before the king, do you think this process became easier or more difficult for her? Why or why not?

- Which of these qualities do you think grew the most in Esther through this repeated process: courage, self-confidence, confidence in the king's willingness to give her whatever she asked, confidence in God to protect her and deliver her people?

With the seal of the king's signet ring, the edict could not be taken back. However, now, Mordecai has the ring. Not only does it give Mordecai, a Jew, power and influence, but it also physically and symbolically demonstrates the reversal of the outcomes of Haman and Mordecai. Yet, Jews across the vast Persian kingdom were still in danger of death and the Persians still empowered to wipe out the entire Jewish race.

- How could an irrevocable decree of the king be revoked? (Literally it could not be revoked. It could only be amplified or qualified in such a way that it superseded or altered the terms of the original, or in Esther's request, "overruling" [8:5] the dispatches from Haman. Hence the royal secretaries were summoned to craft the new document.)

The king passed off, for whatever reason, the job of writing the first edict to Haman and the writing of the second edict to Mordecai, rather than dictating it himself.

- When it comes to using the power of the ring, what is the difference between the king, Haman, and Mordecai?

Invite someone to read Esther 8:9-13, then discuss the following,

A second edict goes out.

Insight

When we compare Haman's hateful edict with the counter-edict written by Mordecai, we note one important difference. Haman called for the destruction of the entire Jewish race. The instructions were to destroy, kill, and annihilate ALL Jews, regardless of age or gender. In contrast, Mordecai called for the protection and defense of the Jews. He directed that only those who attacked the Jews should be killed—armed forces of any nationality. This would include only adult males who demonstrated that they were enemies of the Jews.

Connect to My Life and the World

- How did this second edict provide a way out of the dilemma for the Jews? (It permitted the Jews to defend themselves, and to destroy anyone who did attack them.)

Esther and Mordecai had to take it upon themselves to overturn the law of the land.

- What should believers do when the law of the land violates God's law?

The response of the Jewish people to the second edict was happiness, joy, gladness, honor, feasting, and celebrating (vv. 16-17).

- Share about how you responded to a time when God worked a "reversal" in a circumstance you were facing—bringing a positive outcome from a negative situation you were experiencing.

Haman is repeatedly identified as "Haman the Agagite," "Haman, the enemy of the Jews," and "Haman, son of Hammedatha, the Agagite." There was no forgetting that generations of enmity existed between the descendants of the Amalekites and the Jews.

- Is it easier to forget or to forgive? Why?

- What kinds of prejudice have you seen handed down through generations? (political biases, racial prejudice, personal grudges between families, religious prejudices)

"Prejudice" literally means to pre-judge based on our own mindset without the facts.

- How well do we identify our own prejudices? What can we do to change them?

Although Esther and Mordecai achieved physical safety, wealth, influence, and power, we must not forget that they were still living in exile.

- What kinds of exile separate people groups today? (People displaced by war, famine, and natural disasters. Persons estranged from one another—spouses, friends, children and parents. Prisoners incarcerated long or short-term. Addicts exiled by substances from families, jobs, and dignity. Homeless exiled without a choice from rental properties or family homes. Foster children taken to a whole new world.)

- How would you define an "emotional exile"?

- How do you think people in exile find peace, hope, and reconciliation?

- An intended outcome of this session is that we cooperate with God to bring about deliverance. Are we really connecting to these people in exile if all we do is talk about their needs?

- What overt physical acts of service and compassion are within our power, collectively or individually, to deliver hope to the hopeless?

- Are you living in some type of "exile"? What kind of help do you need? How can we pray for you?

Close with a prayer for exiles and for your group's participation with God to reach out to them.

God in the Shadows

Session Outcome

To value and participate in celebration of God's redemptive work in this world.

Customize:

Daniel is the password to access expanded teaching helps on FoundryLeader.com

Discover:

Illustrated Bible Life reminds us of the importance of remembrance in the celebrations of the church, and provides verse-by-verse commentary on the Scripture passage.

November

24

CELEBRATING GOD'S MERCY

God's people should remember and celebrate important moments of God's amazing mercy and grace.

THE WORD

ESTHER 9:20-32

Mordecai recorded these events, and he sent letters to all the Jews throughout the provinces of King Xerxes, near and far, ²¹to have them celebrate annually the fourteenth and fifteenth days of the month of Adar ²²as the time when the Jews got relief from their enemies, and as the month when their sorrow was turned into joy and their mourning into a day of celebration. He wrote them to observe the days as days of feasting and joy and giving presents of food to one another and gifts to the poor.

²³So the Jews agreed to continue the celebration they had begun, doing what Mordecai had written to them. ²⁴For Haman son of Hammedatha, the Agagite, the enemy of all the Jews, had plotted against the Jews to destroy them and had cast the pur (that is, the lot) for their ruin and destruction. ²⁵But when the plot came to the king's attention, he issued written orders that the evil scheme Haman had devised against the Jews should come back onto his own head, and that he and his sons should be impaled on poles. ²⁶(Therefore these days were called Purim, from the word pur.) Because of everything written in this letter and because of what they had seen and what had happened to them, ²⁷the Jews took it on themselves to establish the custom that they and their descendants and all who join them should without fail observe these two days every year, in the way prescribed and at the time appointed. **²⁸These days should be remembered and observed in every generation by every family, and in every province and in every city. And these days of Purim should never fail to be celebrated by the Jews—nor should the memory of these days die out among their descendants.**

KEY VERSE

Last Week:

We learned the way God's people are called to cooperate with God's plan for deliverance.

This Week:

We will learn the reasons why believers have every reason in the world to celebrate God's grace daily.

Session 13

²⁹So Queen Esther, daughter of Abihail, along with Mordecai the Jew, wrote with full authority to confirm this second letter concerning Purim. ³⁰And Mordecai sent letters to all the Jews in the 127 provinces of Xerxes' kingdom—words of goodwill and assurance— ³¹to establish these days of Purim at their designated times, as Mordecai the Jew and Queen Esther had decreed for them, and as they had established for themselves and their descendants in regard to their times of fasting and lamentation. ³²Esther's decree confirmed these regulations about Purim, and it was written down in the records.

ENGAGE THE WORD

In Exodus, the Israelites are commanded to observe the Passover every year to remember that God delivered them out of Egypt. It is to be a time to remember all God has done for His people; it is a time to celebrate God's mighty acts and look forward to how He will act in the future. Throughout the Bible, the call to God's people is always to remember. To remember who they belong to, to remember what their God has done.

A TIME OF REMEMBERING

Esther 9:20-32

Advent is a season of expectant waiting in the rhythms of the Christian liturgical year, a time where the people of God wait in anticipation for the celebration of Jesus' coming, "God with us" (Matthew 1:23). Seasons of the church help communities reflect on the most important seasonal rhythms of life, reflecting on how these ancient stories of God continue to give life and sustain the church in creative and vibrant ways through these celebratory rhythms. The church needs to remember the ways and wonders of God as it engages with present realities and struggles.

Here in Esther, a difficult space of waiting ensues. Haman has been dealt with, but the edict to destroy the Jews could not be revoked. Esther and Mordecai proceed to intervene in this perilous space and create a counter edict that enables the Jews to defend themselves against armed attackers. As we witnessed in

🔊 **Listen:**

FoundryLeader.com: What are the main holy days on the Christian calendar and how did they develop? That's the focus of this week's *Illustrated Bible Life* "Article Out Loud."

Notes:

_____

_____

_____

_____

_____

_____

_____

_____

_____

_____

_____

_____

_____

_____

_____

Did You Know?

One of the earliest accounts of Purim is from 2 Maccabees (late second century BC). Unlike other pilgrimage festivals commanded in the Torah (e.g., Passover and the Festival of Unleavened Bread, Festival of Weeks, Festival of Tabernacles), no sacrifice or offerings are commanded. Its origin is attributed to the book of Esther.

the previous session, the Lord makes a way for God's people to overcome the enemies of God's kingdom.

Here in Esther 9, the Jews take a stand against those seeking their harm. The Jews were not alone in their defense! "No one could stand against them, because the people of all the other nationalities feared them. And all the nobles of the provinces, the satraps, the governors and the king's administrators helped the Jews, because fear of Mordecai had seized them" (Esther 9:2b-3). The great reversal of Haman's original plot to impale Mordecai now takes an even greater turn of events as Mordecai is "growing powerful" (Esther 9:4b). As the fighting ensues, notice that Haman's edict in Esther 3 allowed for the enemies to take spoils from the Jews. Mordecai's counter edict allows for this as well. This is routine in ancient warfare. As you read through Esther 9, notice that the Jews were permitted by the edict to take spoils after triumphing over their attackers; even so, the text says that the Jews "did not lay hands on the spoil" (Esther 9:10b). They protected themselves, but did not seek economic gain from the situation.

Esther will seek to make another request before the king. This adds a comedic element to the story as the reader is aware that Esther shall be given whatever she asks for! She has the king's favor and this will enable her to seek favor on behalf of the Jewish people once more. Her request is in two parts, (1) an extension of one day for the Jews in Susa to defend themselves and (2) for Haman's 10 sons to be impaled on poles. This public display serves as a warning to any sectors of resistance who seek to harm the Jewish people.

The bold request of Queen Esther results in the Jewish community of Persia being saved! In order to remember the events, the festival of Purim is established and celebrated every year (Esther 9:20-28).

"These days should be remembered and observed in every generation by every family, and in every province

 **Discover:**

Calendars help us remember. The annual observation of birthdays and anniversaries enables us to recall the past and set aside space and time to celebrate life's joys and grieve its losses. Marking time to remember is also a key theme in Christian faith and spirituality. Our Christian calendar helps us to recall the important events of our faith. This week's *Illustrated Bible Life* article explores all the ways in which Christians are "Keeping Holy Time."

Notes:

_____

_____

_____

_____

_____

Session 13

Think About It

As you enter the Advent season this year, how are you preparing your heart as a place of waiting *and* welcoming? Romans 15:7 encourages us to "Welcome one an- other, therefore, just as Christ has welcomed you, for the glory of God" (NRSV).

and in every city. And these days of Purim should never fail to be celebrated by the Jews—nor should the memory of these days die out among their descendants" (Esther 9:28).

Purim derives from the Persian word, *pur*, meaning "lots" or "lottery." (Haman cast lots to decide which day his violent edict would be carried out. See Esther 9:24.) Purim is a festival to celebrate how the Jews obtained "rest" from their enemies and victory over their foes. Purim is celebrated by feasts (eating and drinking), giving gifts, and displays of rejoicing! Today, Purim is still celebrated in a carnivalesque manner with costumes, merry making, special foods, and gifts.

Throughout the Old Testament, God invites Israel to "remember." The Ten Words (commandments) in Exodus 20 begin with God reminding Israel that God brought them out of Egypt. A few verses down, God invites Israel to "remember the Sabbath" (Exodus 20:8).

Remembering our story as God's people through the liturgical year is not just something good to do, but it is essential in recalling our story and remember- ing our identity as God's people. More than reminisc- ing, celebrating the works of God continues to root us in our true identity as God's holy people, a people God has created, loves, and sends into this world to share the good news! It is too easy to forget who we are and whose we are; therefore, let us always remember!

REFLECT | In what ways do you remember and celebrate important moments of God's amazing mercy and grace?

JENNIFER MATHENY

_____

_____

_____

_____

_____

_____

_____

_____

_____

_____

_____

_____

Discussion Guide

Connect to My Experience

Today we're going to look at a Jewish festival that was established and first observed in the book of Esther. *Purim* was created/established to celebrate deliverance of Jews during Persian exile. It is still a major Jewish holiday today.

There are four main Purim rituals (based on Esther 9:22), which are easily compared to some of our holiday rituals today. Name a coordinating aspect of our celebration of Advent or Christmas traditions for each Purim ritual.

1. *Reading the full account of Esther written in scroll format twice, once on the first evening of Purim and again on the next day.* (Christians read the prophecy and events of the birth of Christ in worship services, pageants, around the Christmas family table, etc.)

2. *Giving gifts to the poor.* (December is characteristically compassionate ministry month when Christians donate funds, supplies, and gifts for the poor and disadvantaged.)

3. *Delivering food gifts to at least one person.* (Our compassionate outreach includes giving to food distribution centers and delivering food baskets to needy families.)

4. *Enjoying a Purim feast together.* (It wouldn't be Christmas without everyone around the table for Christmas dinner.)

■ Why do you think these Christian and Jewish holidays have so much in common?

Transition:

Today we celebrate the goodness of God—in the Old Testament, the New Testament, and today—to bring deliverance from evil and sin for all of us.

Connect to the Word

Invite someone to read Esther 9:20-32, then discuss the following,

We do not know for certain who the author of the book of Esther is, but 9:20 suggests it might be Mordecai.

■ Why do you think Mordecai, a Jew in exile, could be the one to record the events, to send the record to all Jews in Persia, and to announce the establishment of a major Jewish holiday in existence to this day? (Not until toward the end of the story does Mordecai increase in power and authority through his new relationship with the king. He earned the king's trust and respect, but God placed him in this role.)

■ How was Purim to be observed? (It was to be two days of feasting and joy, with the giving of presents and food to one another [vv. 19, 22].)

■ What consideration were they to give to others at the Feast of Purim? (They were to give gifts to the poor [v. 22].)

■ How often was the Feast of Purim to be celebrated? (Every year, in every generation, by every family, in every province, and in every city [v. 28].)

■ What was to be the primary purpose of Purim? (Joyful celebration of turning sorrow into joy and mourning into celebration.) What mandatory rituals were to be observed each Purim? (9:22)

■ Why is it important that the Jewish people never fail to celebrate Purim throughout their history? (God's deliverance for the Jews is to be remembered and observed in every generation by every family so that the memory of these days never dies out among their descendants [9:28].) Could there be a possibility to forget this event? If so, how? (Without passing it down from

Insight

At the root of "rehearse" is the Old French word *rehercier*, which has two very interesting meanings for our study—"go over again" and "rake and turn over the soil." To rehearse is to go over and over a presentation until it is memorized and perfected. Deuteronomy 6:7-9 says of God's commandments that we are to "impress" (NIV) or "rehearse" (GNV) them coming and going, waking and sleeping, over and over and over to our children. When this has been forgotten, it's time to "rake and turn over the soil"— actively planting the Word in the hearts of a new generation. A great deal of rehearsing is necessary for remembering and never forgetting.

Connect to My Life and the World

generation to generation in an annual reminder, the story of God's intervention could very easily be lost these 2,500 years later.)

■ What do you think it means to rehearse the things of God? (See **Insight**.)

■ How can rehearsing be understood as a spiritual discipline, such as fasting, solitude, Bible study, prayer, and meditation? Should we rehearse every day, as we do with Bible study or prayer? What form would that take in your daily life?

The crisis is over. People have been obedient to God and risked themselves. God has acted. The story seems to be over. But it isn't. The story is never over unless we forget. We are to remember with gratitude. Traditions and holidays help us to remember—to celebrate—to retell the story of God's faithfulness. That is why we have holidays. And that is why Mordecai instituted Purim. And why Jews still celebrate it.

■ What is our role in collective memory of keeping the stories of God alive?

■ What elements of our own history, both national and spiritual, or our family history of God's intervention are in danger of being forgotten by succeeding generations? How might we be failing God and our children by unintended omission?

We have been focusing on recognizing God's mighty acts in our lives, focusing on the importance of remembering and retelling what God has done. The Feast of Purim is another reminder of the importance of remembering and retelling.

■ What traditions are important to you?

■ Do you have family traditions that have spiritual significance for you? If so what are these?

■ How can we use family traditions as times to celebrate and share God's goodness?

■ How can we use them as an opportunity to do good for others?

■ To what extent can we keep our seasonal observances of holidays (and even holy days) from degenerating from their original purposes?

■ How do we we teach a new generation the values of looking back on what God has done for us and how Jesus' life, death, and resurrection have enabled us to have eternal life?

Although our scripture for today is celebratory in victory, a period of anxious waiting had to be endured first. Xerxes' kingdom was at its time the largest empire the world had seen. Its borders stretched from Egypt to India, encompassing 2.1 million square miles divided into 127 provinces. It would take time for the word of the second edict to reach every corner of the Persian Empire.

■ What makes waiting hard? How are waiting and worrying often intertwined?

■ What can we do while we wait for God to act? (Look back on—rehearse—His faithful intervention. Look forward to His coming answer—His everlasting faithfulness to see you through.)

■ How will today's story affect your embrace of the Advent Season?

Close in prayer.

MATERIALS AVAILABLE

For the leader:

Leader's Guide—one for each leader and assistant leader.

Illustrated Bible Life—background articles/commentary; one for each leader and assistant leader.

Bible Teaching Maps—one for each group.

For the adult participant:

Bible Study Guide—one for each adult in your group. (Also available in large print.)

Standard—take-home Christian leisure-reading magazine; one for each adult.

Reflecting God—daily devotions based on scriptures and themes found in *Adult Faith Connections.* One per household. (Also available in large print.)

Mike L. Wonch
   Editor

Cover Photo: © Daniel _Key/Shutterstock.com

A Year at a Glance . . .

WINTER 2024-25

Unit 1: Isaiah: A Message of Warning and Hope

The book of Isaiah contains a message of warning and judgment, but also a message of hope and redemption. During this unit, we will see how this prophet's overall message points to God's brighter future for those who walk the path of faith.

Unit 2: Life-Changing Encounters with Jesus

We will look at five stories of people whose lives were changed when they encountered the transforming power and presence of Jesus, the Messiah.

SPRING 2025

Unit 1: Who Is Jesus?

Jesus asked His disciples, "Who do you say I am?" (Matthew 16:15). This is a question we must still answer today. During this study, we will see who Jesus is, and rejoice that all of God's promises are fully realized in Jesus.

Unit 2: The Message of Galatians

Paul was concerned for the believers in Galatia. This church was dealing with understanding the relationship between old covenant Judaism and new covenant Christianity, as well as many other questions that needed answering. During this unit, we will examine Paul's letter to the Galatians.

SUMMER 2025

Unit 1: The Wisdom of Proverbs

The wisdom in Proverbs provides practical teaching for our spiritual journey. In this study, we will examine some of the great wisdom passages to discover new insights for our walk with God.

Unit 2: End Things

Since the New Testament was written, people have been fascinated with end times. Through this study, we will look at what the Bible has to say about end things and how to apply these biblical passages today.

Unit 3: What the Bible Says About . . .

Although written thousands of years ago, the Bible still speaks to current culture. In this unit, we will explore what Scripture teaches about politics, gossip, family, and sharing our faith and how to live holy lives in response to those truths.

FALL 2025

Unit 1: Living into God's Promises

God delivered the people out of Egypt, leading them toward the promised land. During this unit, we will not only examine how God prepared His people to enter the promised land, we will also discover the ways God leads people today to claim His promises for their lives.